OSMTJ

KNIGHTS TEMPLAR OF AMERICA

INTRODUCTORY MANUAL

D1520195

OSMTJ Knights Templar of America Introductory Manual
By OSMTJ Knights Templar of America
Ordre Souverain et Militaire du Temple de Jérusalem
Knights Templar of America
Grand Priory of the United States

Published by the Authority of Bryant Jones,
Grand Prior of the United States of America

Various Contributors including:
Bryant Jones, Grand Prior of the United States of America
Sir Bob Zalner, Grand Secretary
Sir Trey Emery, Grand Turcopolier
Sir Alan Scarlett, Prior of Holy Cross
Rev. Timothy Weddell
Knight Commander Daniel J. Clausen, Editor–Contributor
Copyright 2019

A Codex Spiritualis Publication.
Printed in the United States of America.

ISBN–13: 9781726667616

The OSMTJ is a wholly owned ministry of Templar Church, (TemplarChurch.org). Templar Church is a legally constituted church in the USA and incorporated in the state of New Hampshire with Business ID: 725359
Templar Church is a non–profit organization and all donations to Templar Church or it's ministries are tax deductible.

Library of Congress data is available for this title.

Table of Contents

Who We Are

The United States Grand Priory of Ordre Souverain et Militaire du Temple de Jérusalem was founded in 1973 by Father Philip Guarino with the permission and appointment of then Grand Master Antoine Zdrojewski and Swiss Grand Prior Alfred Zappelli.

We are part of the international order, OSMTJ (OSMTJ.net). "OSMTJ" is the French acronym for, "Ordre Souverain et Militaire du Temple de Jérusalem." The United States Grand Priory translates its name into English as: "The Supreme Military Order of the Jerusalem Temple." Our Order strives to the highest ideals and derives its inspiration from the ancient Order of the Temple. Although no group can claim direct descendence from the ancient Order, we strive to be the spiritual and philosophical heirs to the ancient Knights Templar founded by Hugues de Payens in 1118. Our Grand Masters are elected and serve for life, just as it has been done since the beginning of the Order. The position of Grand Master can not be passed on through anyone's will or by being the son of a Grand Master. Any, so called, "Templar" Order that uses those claims to support Grand Master succession is not legitimate. Our Grand Master is His S.E., Master of the Order, General Ronald Mangum.

The Order came into semi-public view in Versailles, France in 1705, when a Convent General of the Order elected the Philippe, Duke of Orleans, later Regent of France, to the Grand Mastership of the Order. Our Order was then restored by His Imperial Majesty, Napoleon Bonaparte, by imperial decree in 1807. In 1853, it was given recognition by Emperor Napoleon III. In 1918, the Order was re-registered in France in accordance with French law. On January 19th,

1932, it was registered in Brussels, Belgium: 1957 Namur / Belgium BE–410 20708. This recording was done by three Belgian Templars in Brussels, Joseph Cleeremans, Gustave Jonckbloedt and Théodore Covias. The record of the registration of the "Sovereign Military Order of the Temple of Jerusalem" appears in the Belgian Monitor on January 20, 1933. Lastly, our Order was re–registered in Namur, Belgium, on November 15th, 1975.

Vision of the Knights Templar of America

The OSMTJ Grand Priory of America, existing for the pure motives of spreading the love of Christ, takes pride in its existence, and pride in its members' involvement in shaping our Nation.

Men and women have been drawn to our Order because freedom, equality, respect, charity, a belief in Jesus Christ.

Men and women of such caliber have made a mark on our societies and still do. The continuous need to face the challenges in today's world in a moral and ethical way is as important now as it was one two hundred and forty years ago when our nation was founded.

The Knights Templar are more than an organization to which you can say you belong to, it is a way of life.

The goal of the Knights Templar to live for Christ, improve ourselves, our families and our communities, is the reason we remain an essential component of the structure of any stable society.

What We Are Not

1. We will never be primarily a fund raising organization. Although we will have small and limited fund drives, this will never be our purpose. Instead our purpose is to build a fraternal Christian community to help and encourage each other along our path in life.

Like our ancient Templar ancestors, we are here to help pilgrims on their road.

2. We will never be a rich order of wealth and power. We strive to be the "Poor Knights of Christ." Our target membership is not the rich and famous but the faithful from every walk of life. Dues are intentionally kept low to allow for the broadest possible participation. Current rates are $65 initial donation, $25 yearly thereafter.

3. We are not a military veteran's club and you will never need to have a military background to be promoted. We are not a militia and we are not preparing for physical warfare. Our focus is preparing men and women to engage and advance in a world where spiritual warfare is constant at a time when much of the church has gone to sleep.

4. We are non–Masonic and are not affiliated at all with Freemasonry.

5. We are not a replacement for your church. To the contrary. Everything we do is geared towards empowering men and women to get off the sidelines in local ministry and become engaged. We encourage our Knights, Sergeants and Companion at Arms, Squires, Chaplains and Chaplain Assistants to mentor members of their local church and community in the love and fealty to our Lord Jesus Christ.

6. We are not bogged down by issues of doctrine. We focus on Jesus Christ and who He is. There is no requirement of any member to abandon their church's doctrine, but we are connected by what unites us as the ecumenical body of Christ.

7. We are not political. While we encourage our members to engage in politics in their personal lives, our Order does not endorse candidates.

8. We are not a secret society. We don't have any secrets to keep and don't use secret oaths. We strive to be transparent and you can read everything about our Order openly.

What We Are

A CHRISTIAN COMMUNITY

Ever wonder why we refer to accepted Knights as Brothers and Sisters? We are building a community of Christians that is deeper than a fraternal Order. Unfortunately, Christians in America have too often settled for polite or friendly relationships in the church when the New Testament holds out a vision for a much richer connection between Christians. We are trying to learn how to love one another with gracious, committed love expressing our family relationship as brothers and sisters in Christ that is more like a family than an organization.

ECUMENICAL: Protestants, Catholics, & Orthodox

While we are members of many churches and Christian traditions, we recognize one another as members of God's family. Thus, brothers and sisters in Christ who seek to be an answer to Jesus's prayer that "they would all be one, Father, just as you are in me and I am in you." John 17:21

THE POOR KNIGHTS OF CHRIST

We strive to be the "Poor Knights of Christ," by including those who can't afford most fraternal orders. "The King will reply, 'Truly I tell you, whatever you did for one of the least of these brothers and sisters of mine, you did for me." – Matthew 25:4. Not everyone knows that the the Knights Templar were originally knows as the Poor Knights of Christ and of the Temple of Solomon because of their strict vows of poverty. We strive to recapture the meaning behind this name and make it a reality for our Order.

HELPING PERSECUTED CHRISTIANS

Like the ancient Templars protected persecuted Christian pilgrims

9

on the road to Jerusalem, our mission is to help persecuted Christians wherever their road may be taking them in life. We are especially called to help Christians in the Middle East. Christians continued to be the most persecuted group across the globe in 2016, according to a study.[1]

The report from Italian–based Center for Studies on New Religions, determined that 90,000 Christians were killed for their beliefs worldwide last year and nearly a third were at the hands of Islamic extremists like ISIS.

Others were killed by state and non–state persecution, including in places like North Korea. "U.S. policy has not had a strategy for specifically addressing the persecution of Christians," Ryan Mauro, national security analyst for the Clarion Project told FoxNews.com "For example, very few people are even aware that Iraqi Christians began organizing to defend themselves and needed our help." The study also found that as many as 600 million Christians were prevented from practicing their faith in 2016.

We stand with and support these persecuted brothers and sisters through established and focused ministries such as OpenDoors USA and Voice of the Martyrs.

---

1   See: http://www.foxnews.com/world/2017/01/06/christians–most–persecuted–group–in–world–for–second–year–study.html

What We Believe

The Ordre Souverain et Militaire du Temple de Jérusalem is a multi–denominational ministry (Catholic, Protestant, and Orthodox). All of our members, regardless of personal choice of worship, style of ministry, or doctrinal beliefs, have agreed to the following creeds as expressions of our faith and for organizational and ministerial unity.

* Please note when the word "catholic" is used in any of these creeds, it's not referring to the Catholic church but merely the universal, world–wide church.

Apostle's Creed

I believe in God the Father, Almighty, Maker of heaven and earth:And in Jesus Christ, his only begotten Son, our Lord:
Who was conceived by the Holy Ghost, born of the Virgin Mary:
Suffered under Pontius Pilate; was crucified, dead and buried:
He descended into hell:
The third day he rose again from the dead:
He ascended into heaven, and sits at the right hand of God the Father Almighty:
From thence he shall come to judge the quick and the dead:
I believe in the Holy Ghost:
I believe in the holy catholic church: the communion of saints:
The forgiveness of sins:
The resurrection of the body:
And the life everlasting.
Amen.

The Nicene Creed

We believe in one God, the Father, the Almighty, maker of heaven and earth, of all that is, seen and unseen.

We believe in one Lord, Jesus Christ, the only Son of God, eternally begotten of the Father,

God from God, Light from Light, true God from true God, begotten, not made, of one Being with the Father.

Through him all things were made.

For us and for our salvation, he came down from heaven: by the power of the Holy Spirit

He became incarnate from the Virgin Mary, and was made man.

For our sake he was crucified under Pontius Pilate; he suffered death and was buried.

On the third day he rose again in accordance with the Scriptures;

He ascended into heaven and is seated at the right hand of the Father.

He will come again in glory to judge the living and the dead, and his kingdom will have no end.

We believe in the Holy Spirit, the Lord, the giver of life, who proceeds from the Father and the Son.

With the Father and the Son he is worshiped and glorified. He has spoken through the Prophets.

We believe in one holy catholic and apostolic Church. We acknowledge one baptism for the forgiveness of sins.

We look for the resurrection of the dead, and the life of the world to come.

Amen.

Athanasian Creed

Whosoever will be saved, before all things it is necessary that he hold the universal faith;

Which faith except every one do keep whole and undefiled,

without doubt he shall perish everlastingly.

And the catholic faith is this: That we worship one God in Trinity, and Trinity in Unity;

Neither confounding the persons nor dividing the substance.

For there is one person of the Father, another of the Son, and another of the Holy Spirit.

But the Godhead of the Father, of the Son, and of the Holy Spirit is all one, the glory equal, the majesty coeternal.

Such as the Father is, such is the Son, and such is the Holy Spirit.

The Father uncreated, the Son uncreated, and the Holy Spirit uncreated.

The Father incomprehensible, the Son incomprehensible, and the Holy Spirit incomprehensible.

The Father eternal, the Son eternal, and the Holy Spirit eternal.

And yet they are not three eternals but one eternal.

As also there are not three uncreated nor three incomprehensible, but one uncreated and one incomprehensible.

So likewise the Father is almighty, the Son almighty, and the Holy Spirit almighty.

And yet they are not three almighties, but one almighty.

So the Father is God, the Son is God, and the Holy Spirit is God;

And yet they are not three Gods, but one God.

So likewise the Father is Lord, the Son Lord, and the Holy Spirit Lord;

And yet they are not three Lords but one Lord.

For like as we are compelled by the Christian verity to acknowledge every Person by himself to be God and Lord;

So are we forbidden by the catholic religion to say; There are three Gods or three Lords.

The Father is made of none, neither created nor begotten.

The Son is of the Father alone; not made nor created, but begotten.

The Holy Spirit is of the Father and of the Son; neither made, nor created, nor begotten, but proceeding.

So there is one Father, not three Fathers; one Son, not three Sons; one Holy Spirit, not three Holy Spirits.

And in this Trinity none is before or after another; none is greater or less than another.

But the whole three persons are co–eternal, and co–equal.

So that in all things, as aforesaid, the Unity in Trinity and the Trinity in Unity is to be worshipped.

He therefore that will be saved must thus think of the Trinity.

Furthermore it is necessary to everlasting salvation that he also believe rightly the incarnation of our Lord Jesus Christ.

For the right faith is that we believe and confess that our Lord Jesus Christ, the Son of God, is God and man.

God of the substance of the Father, begotten before the worlds; and man of substance of His mother, born in the world.

Perfect God and perfect man, of a reasonable soul and human flesh subsisting.

Equal to the Father as touching His Godhead, and inferior to the Father as touching His manhood.

Who, although He is God and man, yet He is not two, but one Christ.

One, not by conversion of the Godhead into flesh, but by taking of that manhood into God.

One altogether, not by confusion of substance, but by unity of person.

For as the reasonable soul and flesh is one man, so God and man is one Christ;

Who suffered for our salvation, descended into hell, rose again the third day from the dead;

He ascended into heaven, He sits on the right hand of the Father, God, Almighty;

From thence He shall come to judge the quick and the dead.

At whose coming all men shall rise again with their bodies;

and shall give account of their own works.

And they that have done good shall go into life everlasting and they that have done evil into everlasting fire.

This is the catholic faith, which except a man believe faithfully he cannot be saved.

Were the Knights Templar Abolished?

The question a Knight Templar hears often when explaining the Order is, "But didn't the Pope abolish them?" The answer is "no." Here is the explanation:

On Friday, 13 October 1307, government officials throughout France unsealed envelopes containing orders to arrest all members of the Knights Templar on shocking charges, backed up by Papal Edict of heresy, homosexuality, and idol worship. Five years later, at the Council of Vienne in 1312, Pope Clement V issued his bull of suppression of the Order.

So, did the Pope then have the authority to disband the Knights Templar? He did not, because the Pope did not create them – the Knights Templar existed on their own for eleven years before the Pope officially gave them ecclesiastical recognition.

The Order originates from 1118, after the successful capture of Jerusalem in the First Crusade. Joining together to protect Christian pilgrims on their way to the Holy Land, nine French crusader knights led by Hugues de Payens took vows of poverty, chastity, and obedience. King Baldwin II gave the Templars his palace on the south side of the Dome of the Rock. For the next eleven years they grew and continued their job of protecting pilgrims.

The Catholic Church officially endorsed the Knights Templar in 1129 at the Council of Troyes. So all the Pope had authority to do was remove his formal ecclesiastical recognition of the Order because he did not create them. Thus, the Knights Templar still exist today as they did for their first eleven years, without official Catholic Church recognition. Unlike Medieval times, lack of Catholic Church recognition is not necessary for thousands of organizations like ours that do good works independent from the Church.

Nevertheless, on October 25th, 2009, the Vatican released the Chinon parchment, a document that is a summation of the trials that was written shortly after they occurred. The parchment demonstrates and the Catholic Church acknowledged that the Knights Templar were innocent of heresy.

A letter to the Pope from living descendants of the Templars appeared in the press in 2004. It stated: "We shall witness the 700th anniversary of the persecution of our Order on 13th October 2007. It would be just and fitting for the Vatican to acknowledge our grievance in advance of this day of mourning." On 25 October 2007, exactly 13 days from the morning of the anniversary, an official document was released by the Vatican absolving the Knights Templar and confirming their innocence.

Why Modern Knighthood?

When most people think about knights, they think of feudal knights serving a sovereign. Probably the most famous knights in the English speaking world were King Arthur's Knights of the Round Table. These knights served their king and also went on sacred quests to find the Holy Grail. The German writer Wolfram von Eschenbach, in his immortal medieval work Parzifal, equated the Grail Knights with the Knights Templar. Both the Grail Knights of Arthur's realm and the Knights Templar were dedicated to achieving purity of heart: the spiritual attribute that would allow one to have a vision of the Grail—or to see God, as the Beatitudes stated.

The essential quality of knighthood was complete devotion to one's sovereign in the case of secular knights, or complete devotion to Jesus Christ and His church in the case of knights belonging to one of the religious Orders. Knights of both types devoted themselves to skill of arms. Whether religious or secular, however, a knight was expected to be unrelenting in battle, fearless in the face of hopeless odds, and magnanimous in victory.

Knights are not just a thing of the past, however. There are a number of chivalric Orders that exist today. The British monarchy still grants knighthoods, as does the Papacy with the Order of Christ. Two religious Orders that still grant knighthoods are the Knights of Malta (Order of St. John) and this Order, The Ordre Souverain et Militaire du Temple de Jérusalem. In all cases where a secular knighthood is granted, it is for exceptional service to the sovereign or to certain worthwhile causes, while knighthoods granted by religious Orders are in recognition of service to God and one's fellow man.

OSMTJ KNIGHTS TEMPLAR OF AMERICA

The traditional role of the knight was to defend the defenseless, to be pious in worship and in dealings with others, and to maintain one's personal honor above all costs. Such knightly values might seem out of place in the 21st century, with so much emphasis on "me," money, and materialism—but a few individuals still believe life is truly not worth living unless it serves a higher purpose. Such individuals believe that "living a holy life," and not material success, is the most important thing to which we can aspire. These are the kind of men and women that we are seeking to join the Knights Templar!

What are the reasons for having knights in the 21st century?

First, there is the matter of commitment. As opposed to the past, most modern institutions do not ask much in the way of commitment. In the past, people were asked to give more of themselves to the church and to the community; in many cases today, all that we are asked to give is money. There are few things in the modern age that ask for personal loyalty, or that reciprocate loyalty in turn. Seemingly, there is little expectation that people want to commit themselves to anything, or to receive a commitment in return. The man or woman who would become a knight, however, feels unfulfilled in such a world. These men and women are looking for something to give themselves to wholeheartedly, something in which to invest all of their heart, mind, and soul. Just as importantly, they are looking for something that will reciprocate their loyalty and devotion.

Those who become knights know that although there are government agencies and private charities to fight poverty, and military or police to fight the enemies of our country and its citizens, these are not enough. They know that unless good men and good women take personal responsibility for making the world a better place to live, none of the organizations and agencies in existence will be enough to keep the forces of darkness at bay.

Knighthood takes the concept of personal responsibility to the "next level." Knowing that many of their fellow men and women will do nothing, those who aspire to knighthood believe that it is incumbent upon them to do that much more.

One example is poverty. As our Lord said, "The poor you will always have with you." For all of the programs administered by the government, and charities operated by the churches and other organizations, there will always be the poor. We should not, however, let the existence of "programs" give us an excuse for inaction. The true knight has internalized the story about the "Good Samaritan," and helps the poor or disadvantaged whenever he or she can. It is not necessary to always give money—a knight's most precious gift may be his or her time, which may be spent teaching the illiterate how to read, or driving elderly persons to a doctor's appointment. A true knight should never walk past someone who is truly in need without trying to help! Never. That is a knight's creed.

A knight however, is distinguished from those who merely dispense aid to the poor and disadvantaged. That distinguishing feature is the willingness to engage in "knightly combat," the battle against evil.

It will take men and women with the dedication of true knights to make the changes that are needed. It will take men and women with the courage of true knights to stand up and be counted, and to demand accountability from our respective governments on their relations with countries that persecute Christians. It will take men and woman like those of the Ordre Souverain et Militaire du Temple de Jérusalem.

Our Order was founded in 1118 A.D. to protect Christians journeying to and from the Holy Land. Later, the Order was responsible for protecting Christians in the Holy Land itself. We have stayed true to our original charter by defending the persecuted church in foreign lands. Our mission is just as compelling today, if not more so, than it was 886 years ago.

Our Order believes that there is still a place for knights in the 21st century. We believe there will always be a place for knights as long as there is poverty, the needs of the elderly, the sick, the helpless, and the persecution of the church. This is not a question: "Do I have time?" Or, "I will get to that soon." This is not subject to negotiation or scheduling. Fellowship and aid to the less fortunate, the helpless are a Templar's duty, his sworn duty. His code of honor demands the core of knighthood in it's unquestionable obligation to help the poor, the sick, the persecuted, the old, the needy, the helpless, the hungry, the cold, the unprotected. These duties are not stipulations; they are a code gladly taken by a Knight Templar. If one attempts to join our Order merely as a fraternity "club," or for a title, it would never make one a Knight Templar. Being a Knight Templar is not a remnant of the past, it is a current way of life.

Regarding our Warfare
By Knight Commander Rev. Daniel J. Clausen

The Knights Templar were founded as a religious military order in the days when Christians faced a violent threat from Islam. In those days the threat posed by physical oppression was a way of life. Civilization had not yet developed a desire to prevent armed conflict. On the contrary, kings and kingdoms still attempted to expand their territory by force and ideas were frequently suppressed by the sword rather than by the strength of reason.

Today, the fields of battle have changed. Although there is still a threat in the United States of mass shootings by individuals, the days of fielding an army within our own borders is seemingly gone, and should the need arise, it is the task of the secular armed forces to handle such threats. Within our ranks, there may be those who have the skill and training to utilize their second amendment rights to be guardians of the innocent wherever they may venture – may God use them. But one might be left to wonder what the major task of an Order of warrior–monks is under this very different field of threats than what the historical Knights Templar faced?

The first thing we must understand is that though we are not in a physical warfare, we are yet in a battle against many threats in the modern age – and our fight ought to be no less vigorous, courageous or zealous. The threat may change, therefore tactics change, but the fact that we are warriors changes not.

In fact, one could argue that the nature of our current warfare is more Biblically aligned than our historical forebears. Consider the words of the Apostle Paul: *2 Corinthians 10:3 "For though we walk in the flesh, we are not waging war according to the flesh. For the weapons of our warfare are not of the flesh but have divine power to destroy strongholds. We destroy arguments and every lofty opinion raised against the knowledge of God, and take every thought captive to obey Christ."*

The Apostle is clear that the mission of the Christian warrior is not skill against sword, shield, spear, or bow, which may kill the flesh, but against ideas and beliefs that are contrary to God and have the power to kill the soul. These are the real enemies. The true strongholds to siege are not made of stone and mortar, but the entrenched battlements of stubborn unbelief in the hearts of men and in our culture.

Jesus makes it clear to us the one we ought to fear: Matthew 10:28 *"And fear not them which kill the body, but are not able to kill the soul: but rather fear him which is able to destroy both soul and body in hell."* This verse speaks specifically about those who warfare against us, who may persecute us and slay our bodies – they are not to be feared, but rather we fear only our Father in Heaven who has the power over the soul. Classically, knights battled those who could kill the body, but in our age, we battle those who endanger themselves and others with poisonous ideas that are capable of securing themselves the condemnation of their irreligion. It is our compassion that drives us to save them from themselves. It is our mercy that causes us to throw ourselves into the heat of this spiritual melee.

Therefore, those who bear the sword of Atheism, we engage them in a battle of knowledge. If they ride upon the steed of Islam, we set up a spear of reason to meet their charge. We don our armor with the understanding that the very people who bear these convictions are not our enemy themselves, but are rather the weapons employed by our perennial foe, Satan, who like a cruel dictator would use his own populace as human shields against the force of our press.

What does this mean in practical living? First, we must truly and deliberately arm ourselves with knowledge and with prayer for the purpose of engaging our culture and communities with a clear expression of the Gospel. This means we must actually talk to people about the difficult and sensitive topics of religion and belief. We must be trained not only in our Christian ways, but in the ways of the beliefs we oppose. Or do you suppose the Templars were only familiar with their own fighting tactics, and not the strategies of the Fatimids or the Ummayids? We study to show ourselves approved and educate ourselves not only in our arguments, but be prepared for what the world will confront us with.

But do not despair, fellow soldier. Just as a man has apprehension before going into battle, perhaps you have apprehension about engaging in a heavy discussion and debate. Nevertheless, a soldier must fight, and if they fight not, they are no soldier but a deserter, or else a coward. Men pray for their weakness in the trenches, and we must pray for our weakness in our debates. We must prepare for battle to tear down cultural strongholds and every high thing that exalts itself against the knowledge of God. By doing this and training others to do so, we protect the souls of pilgrims on their way to the heavenly Jerusalem.

Furthermore, this requires that we must cultivate fortitude of character by the Holy Spirit to engage in this combat without descending into spite, anger, or pride.

Consider the Holy Armor the Apostle commands us to put on: Eph 6:10–20 *"Finally, my brethren, be strong in the Lord, and in the power of his might. Put on the whole armour of God, that ye may be able to stand against the wiles of the devil. For we wrestle not against flesh and blood, but against principalities, against powers, against the rulers of the darkness of this world, against spiritual wickedness in high places. Wherefore take unto you the whole armour of God, that ye may be able to withstand in the evil day, and having done all, to stand.*

Stand therefore, having your loins girt about with truth, and having on the breastplate of righteousness; And your feet shod with the preparation of the gospel of peace; Above all, taking the shield of faith, wherewith ye shall be able to quench all the fiery darts of the wicked. And take the helmet of salvation, and the sword of the Spirit, which is the word of God: Praying always with all prayer and supplication in the Spirit, and watching thereunto with all perseverance and supplication for all saints; And for me, that utterance may be given unto me, that I may open my mouth boldly, to make known the mystery of the gospel, For which I am an ambassador in bonds: that therein I may speak boldly, as I ought to speak."

If you will note, the entire purpose of the Whole Armor of God is stated with a view to bold utterance to make known the mystery of the Gospel to hostile hearers. It seems that even the great Apostle Paul needed boldness through prayer and donning the Armor – it was not innate for him, it was provided and utilized.

Lastly, when we are not engaged in active warfare, we use the means given to us to bring solace and comfort to those who have been casualties of Satan's wiles. This involves everything from bringing food to the hungry, care for the orphan, prayer for the afflicted. These things we do in our own lives as individuals, corporately within our Priories, and universally as Templars. We use funds to aid persecuted Christians in some of the most difficult places in the world through established missions, such as Voice of the Martyrs.

There is no lack of good a Templar may do if we take this seriously. Resist the temptation to view your Templar life as a club or fraternity. Your warfare is real, present, and pressing all around you. Do your duty, good Templar, and prepare yourself today. And should you wage war today against the Spirit of Anti–Christ which is already in the world, in the great Day of the Lord you may be found worthy to fight alongside our King and His Ten Thousands of Holy Ones as He descends to *"execute judgment upon all, and to convince all that are ungodly among them of all their ungodly deeds which they have ungodly committed, and of all their hard speeches which ungodly sinners have spoken against him."* Jude 1:15.

Not unto us, O Lord, not unto us, but to thy name give the glory.

Statutes of the Ordre Souverain et Militaire du Temple de Jerusalem
An association organized and operating under the law of Switzerland

Preamble: The Order is an autonomous international Christian chivalric organization which traces its heritage to the original Order of the Temple of Jerusalem, founded in Jerusalem circa 1118 A.D. It is founded to support, in the modern world, many of the ideals embodied in the devotion and sacrifice of the knights of the original Order.

While sections of these Statutes are derived from the Primitive Rule of the Templars, the Statutes of 1705 and other extant historical documents of the earlier Order, the present day Order is self-governing, subject to no higher authority than obedience and devotion to Christian chivalric ideals and teachings of Our Lord Jesus Christ, and to the promulgation and spread of those ideals and teachings throughout the world. The Order draws its power to govern from the consent of its member constituent bodies, its Christian strength from religious protectors, and its chivalric authority from royal patrons.

Article I. Title of the Order.

The title of this Organization in French is "Ordre Souverain et Militaire du Temple de Jerusalem" abbreviated "OSMTJ", which when used by its constituent bodies, may be followed by a translation of the title into the national language in use by that body, and hereinafter this Organization shall be called the "Order". The Order is an international cultural Christian and humanitarian organization, organized as an international association of national entities operating under Chapter 210 of federal civil code of Switzerland.

Article II. Objects and Purpose of the Order.

The Order is based on an ancient Christian brotherhood, and its objects and purposes shall be:

a. To provide an opportunity for the practice of ecumenical Christianity to support the precepts of Christian Chivalry and to investigate and emulate the historical ideals of the ancient Order.

b. To encourage and promote Christian humanitarian work and charity generally, and especially in support of oppressed Christian peoples in the Middle East.

c. To encourage all that makes for the spiritual and moral strengthening of humankind in accordance with the first great principle of the Order embodied in its motto:

"Not unto us, O Lord, not unto us, but unto thy name give glory."

d. To form and administer establishments, councils, associations, centers or other subordinate bodies to facilitate the work of the Order in all regions.

e. To maintain contact and develop collaboration with kindred Orders and bodies.

The Order is not organized for profit and no part of the net earnings of the Order shall inure to the benefit of any private member or individual. The Order shall not attempt to influence legislation and shall not participate in any campaign activity for or against political candidates.

Article III.

The official languages of the Order are English, Spanish and French.

Article IV.

The Grand Master, elected by the Grand Magistral Council for a renewable term of ten years, shall be the head of the Order, shall represent the Order at diplomatic and international functions, and shall perform such other duties as may be appropriate to his office.

1. The Grand Master shall make all appointments and shall exercise supreme direction, administrative and executive control over the affairs of the Order, its establishments, its subordinate organizations, and its members. The Grand Master shall have the right to veto any recommendation, resolution, decision or proceeding of the Grand Magistral Council or of any subordinate organization of the Order.

2. In the event of the death or permanent and total disability of the Grand Master, the Grand Chancellor shall assume the role of Regent of the Order and shall, within six months after the death or disability of the Grand Master, organize and conduct an election by the Grand Priors of a new Grand Master. In the absence of such action by the Regent, the Grand Priors by majority vote shall continue the affairs of the Order until a new Grand Master is elected. The Regent shall under the direction of the Grand Magistral Council, conduct the day to day affairs of the Order until a new Grand Master is elected. Such authority may be exercised by the Regent for no longer than six months, and all actions taken by the Regent must be ratified by the Grand Magistral Council as soon as is practicable at a meeting or by mail or electronic polling of its members at any time.

Article V. Structure of the Order.

1. The Order is composed of autonomous Grand Priories. Only one Grand Priory may exist in any one nation or state. Subject to the direction of the Grand Master, the Order is governed by its Grand Priors under the following structures,

2. The Grand Magistral Council which is the supreme Legislative Body of the Order is comprised of the Grand Master and the Grand Priors, with decisional vote, and the Grand Magistral Officers with consultative vote. Any Grand Magistral Officer who is also a serving Grand Prior may only vote once as an officer, however, his Grand Priory may also be represented by his designee who shall cast the vote of the Grand Priory. The Grand Magistral Council shall meet at least one time each year.

3. In the conduct of the international affairs of the Order, The Grand Magistral Council shall have the power, subject to the direction of the Grand Master, to make, amend, revoke or suspend (in whole or in part and either generally or in relation to any specified area) Rules for any purpose expressed in these Statutes or otherwise as it may deem necessary or expedient for the conduct, control or management of the international affairs of the Order and, when published in such manner as the Grand Magistral Council may direct, such Rules shall be binding on all organizations, or persons, to which they are applicable, except that the Grand Magistral Council shall not interfere in the internal affairs of any Grand Priory, Priory or other subordinate organization.

4. To facilitate the conduct of the international affairs and work of the Order, the Grand Magistral Council may, in its discretion and subject to the direction of the Grand Master, delegate in such manner as its deems fit any of its powers and authority to any Grand Magistral Officer, or other officer of the Order as it may specify, provided always that the Grand Magistral Council shall not delegate the Grand Master's authority to make Rules, or to approve recommendations for admission, suspension or expulsion of constituent bodies, members and establishments in the Order.

5. The Grand Magistral Council may appoint Committees of such membership and with such terms of reference as it may specify, or as

prescribed by these Statutes or Rules.

Article VI. The Grand Magistral Officers.

1. Grand Chancellor. The Grand Master shall appoint a Grand Chancellor, who shall serve for a term of three years or at the Pleasure of the Grand Master. The Grand Chancellor shall be the chief operating officer of the Order and shall perform such functions as designated by the Grand Master.

2. The Grand Magistral Council shall elect, for a similar term as the Grand Chancellor, the following officers, in order of precedence, who shall perform the listed duties.

a. **Grand Secretary General,** who shall be appointed by the Grand Chancellor upon ratification of the Grand Magistral Council and shall hold office during the pleasure of the Grand Chancellor or until resignation, shall be responsible for all international administrative matters of the Order.

b. **Grand Treasurer,** who shall be appointed by the Grand Chancellor upon ratification of the Grand Magistral Council and shall hold office during the pleasure of the Grand Chancellor or earlier resignation, and who shall be responsible for all international financial matters of the Order.

c. **Grand Marshal,** who shall be appointed by the Grand Chancellor upon ratification of the Grand Magistral Council, and shall hold office during the pleasure of the Grand Chancellor or earlier resignation, shall prescribe and regulate the arrangements for all ceremonies of the Order in accord with the wishes of the Grand Magistral Council.

d. **Grand Almoner,** who shall be appointed by the Grand Chancellor upon ratification of the Grand Magistral Council, and shall hold office during the pleasure of the Grand Chancellor or earlier resignation, and shall be responsible for the charitable and humanitarian activities of the Order in accord with the wishes of the Grand Magistral Council.

e. **Grand Referendary,** who shall be appointed by the Grand Chancellor upon ratification of the Grand Magistral Council, and shall hold office during the pleasure of the Grand Chancellor or earlier resignation, shall be responsible to deal with any disputes that arise between Grand Magistral Officers, the Magisterium, or Grand Magistral Council and constituent bodies or members of the Order, or members of the public.

f. **Grand Chaplain General,** who shall be a Christian cleric of Bishopric rank, and who shall be appointed by the Grand Chancellor upon ratification of the Grand Magistral Council, and shall hold office during the pleasure of the Grand Chancellor or earlier resignation, shall be the advisor to the Grand Magistral Council in all matters of an ecclesiastical nature and shall determine the form of religious service and prayers to be used on such occasions as are not otherwise provided for in the Statutes or Rules.

3. Special Non-voting Officers.

a. Royal Patrons shall be members of ruling or former ruling royal houses who consent to be Royal Patrons of the Order. The Royal Patrons have honorary duties to advise the Order on affairs of heraldry.

b. Religious Protectors shall be senior Christian religious leaders who l consent toprovide religious protection and guidance to the Order.

4. The Grand Master may appoint other international officers who shall hold office during the pleasure of the Grand Master or until removal or resignation and shall be responsible for such matters as may be referred to them by the Grand Master.

5. After the end of their term of office, each Grand Magistral Officer shall be entitled to retain their title of office followed by the

word "emeritus."

Article VII. The Magisterium.

The Grand Master, Grand Chancellor, Grand Treasurer, and the Grand Secretary General shall be the Magisterium, which as the executive committee of the Order, governs between meetings of the Magisterial Council. The Magisterium meets in person or by electronic means, at the call of the Grand Master and shall consider matters referred to it by the Grand Master, shall make recommendations for action to, and shall implement the decisions of, the Grand Magistral Council.

Article VIII. Establishments of the Order.

The constituent establishments of the Order are autonomous Grand Priories and Priories and those Templar organizations that have agreed to maintain the obligations of membership described in the Statutes and Rules. Each Templar group wishing to become a member of the Order may petition the Grand Master for membership in the Order, and upon acceptance by the Grand Master and upon the recommendation of the Grand Magistral Council, and by its agreement to maintain the obligations of membership described in the Statutes and Rules, shall become a constituent member of the Order.

Article IX. Grades of the Order.

1. The Order recognizes the following Grades:

Grade I Knights and Dames Grand Croix of the Temple (GCTJ/DGCTJ)

Grade II Knights and Dames Grand Officier of the Temple (GOTJ/DOTJ)

Grade III Knights and Dames Commander of the Temple

(KCTJ/DCTJ)

Grade IV Knights and Dames of the Temple (KTJ/DTJ)

2. The postnominals adopted for each Grade may properly be used by those to whom they apply to indicate their grade in the Order in the context of any occasion or matter connected with their participation in the work of the Order, or for inclusion in any publication of a biographical nature but admission, attachment, or promotion to any Grade in the Order, or the privileges derived therefrom of wearing the insignia appertaining or belonging thereto, shall not confer any rank, style, title, dignity, appellation or social precedence whatsoever.

Article X. Promotions in the Order.

Promotion in the Order to Grade I (Grand Croix) shall be conferred only by the Grand Master, a Grand Prior or by the Grand Magistral Council.

Article XI. Foundation, Donations and Oblations.

The Order is devoted to works of charity and humanitarian action, and it is a fundamental rule that those who belong to the Order shall contribute to the extent of their capability to its charitable and humanitarian works such donations and oblations as shall be from time to time established by the Grand Magistral Council. On dissolution of the Order, any amounts remaining, after the payment of debts, will be disposed of by the Grand Magistral Council for such similar Christian charitable causes as it selects.

Article XII. Interpretation and Amendment.

1. In these Statutes, unless the context otherwise requires, words

denoting the masculine include the feminine, words in the singular include the plural and words in the plural include the singular, all as appropriate to the context.

2. If at any time the Grand Magistral Council, in the exercise of the powers conferred upon it, shall ordain that any office or body constituted by or under these Statutes shall have its name changed, any reference to such office or body in these Statutes or in Rules made hereunder shall be read and construed as a reference to such office or body by such new name.

3. If any question arises as to the interpretation of these Statutes, the matter shall be referred to the Grand Master, whose decision shall be final.

Adopted by vote of the Grand Magistral Council effective 1 March, 2020.

Statutes of the Grand Priory of the USA

We hereby set forth the following guiding principles of the OSMTJ (Ordre Souverain et Militaire du Temple de Jérusalem) Grand Priory of America, in order to reaffirm the charter of our founders, and to ensure that our Grand Priory is never corrupted or compromised in its principles. As the OSMTJ Grand Priory of America has entered the Third Millennium after the advent of our Lord, we hold the following articles indefeasible and central to the legitimacy and continued survival of the Grand Priory of America:

Article I

We forever dedicate ourselves to the service of our Lord Jesus Christ, and the universal, Holy Christian Church that He founded. We are an ecumenical Christian Grand Priory, with admission open to all professing Christians, Catholics, Protestants, and Orthodox, regardless of church affiliation or denomination. We look forward to the day when all Christian churches are once again unified, and until that time pledge ourselves to act as a bridge between the various denominations and congregations of the universal Christian church.

Article II

As a Christian Grand Priory, we singularly worship and serve our Lord Jesus Christ. We believe in God the Eternal Father and in His Son, Jesus Christ, and in the Holy Ghost, as professed by our Lord and preached by His Apostles. We therefore restrict entry into the Order to baptized Christians, eighteen years of age or older, except that the sixteen–year–old or sons and daughters of Dames and Knights may also be granted full membership. We cannot hold any deities of other religions as equal to our Lord, nor grant membership in the Grand Priory to those who do.

Article III

We decry all occult beliefs and practices, declaring them to be anathema and forbidden to all those in the OSMTJ Grand Priory of America. Any Templar who engages in other than Christian worship is automatically excommunicated from the Grand Priory of America, and will be formally expelled.

Article IV

As a Grand Priory, we will never embrace any sectarian cause or political party, other than concerns oaths of fealty or allegiance those countries hosting our priories. While individual knights and dames are free to hold their own opinions and to take part in the political process, they must never associate the Grand Priory with any sectarian or political cause, no matter how noble, lest this Grand Priory be identified with that cause and it detract from our holy purposes. We are dedicated to fostering the rights of Christians in all lands to worship freely, and we consider activities in support of this cause to be more spiritual than secular, as outlined in Article XII.

Article V

No officer or official in the OSMTJ Grand Priory of America will ever order a subordinate knight or dame to perform any act or duty that violates his or her conscience, or religious beliefs, to include the canon law of his or her church, or the laws of his or her country, or applicable international law.

Article VI

We are bound to uphold all just and moral oaths, such as oaths of fealty, and marriage or sacerdotal vows, but no secret oath shall ever be required in the OSMTJ Grand Priory of America. Nor will blood oaths ever be required of a member of this Grand Priory, for our Lord is the ultimate Judge of whether or not a just and moral oath has been truly kept and fulfilled. All oaths taken by a Knight Templar will be taken on the Christian Bible.

Article VII

We hold, now and forever, that neither titles nor ranks shall ever be for sale, nor will entry into the Grand Priory of America ever be dependent upon any person's financial or social status. Nor will any knight or dame ever be dismissed from the Grand Priory or held in contempt for the inability to pay dues or obligations. Neither shall any priory nor other governing body of our organization ever levy involuntary assessments on any knight or dame. As the true and spiritual descendants of the original "Poor Knights of Christ," we will never value money or other material things over humble service to our Lord.

Article VIII

All priories that make up the Grand Priory of America shall remain autonomous, but shall recognize and honor those officers elected to serve as the governing body of the Confederation, insofar as no magisterial decrees or other orders issued by the Confederation may conflict with this Declaration, the statutes of the Confederation, the laws of the land, or applicable international law.

Article IX

In the case of any priory that violates this Declaration, the statutes of the Confederation of the Grand Priory of America, or the bylaws of the priory itself, in that such a priory may have departed from Templar principles and operates in such a manner as to bring dishonor and discredit upon our Grand Priory, the Secretary General of the Confederation may call for a vote of expulsion by all the member priories, and may expel the offending priory from the Confederation, and declare it no longer part of this Grand Priory, upon a unanimous vote by all the Priors of the other member priories.

Article X

We recognize all other legitimate Knights Templar Orders, and we seek to ally ourselves with other true Knights Templar Orders, but we do not recognize, nor admit the existence of any Templar Order with a superior claim to that of our own.

Article XI

The Grand Priory of America may, from time to time, select a Royal or spiritual Protector for the Grand Priory, and shall pay homage to the same; however, the selection of a Royal or spiritual protector will not imply or express an elevation of the protector's church over any other church body. We also hereby ordain that all members of the Grand Priory shall render the proper respect to all Christian churches and their lawful clerics and leaders, and will never seek to cause division or schism in the Grand Priory due to theological differences between the various churches and their congregations. We also give grateful thanks to the churches that have assisted this Grand Priory in its time of need.

Article XII

Whereas the Knights Templar were originally founded to protect the Christian pilgrims traveling to the Holy Land, we hold as one of our most sacred duties to be an advocate for the right of Christians to worship freely wherever they may reside or travel, and we will not rest until all Christians are accorded this basic God–given right. We hereby pledge our knightly honor as defenders of the faith, as we pray that our Grand Priory may once again fulfill its charge to guard the sacred places in the Holy Land.

Article XIII

The OSMTJ Grand Priory of America will never reject any postulant on the basis of race, sex, ethnic origins, nationality, social, economic, or educational status, political creed, or Christian tradition. We hold that in addition to being a baptized Christian and a person of good character, the chief criterion for acceptance will be the postulant's willingness to serve the Grand Priory faithfully and without thought of recompense. We similarly hold that no postulant has an automatic right to join the Grand Priory, but must be accepted by the membership of the priory to which he or she has applied, and meet the standards established for membership in the Grand Priory.

Article XIV

We hold that beneath our white mantles that we are all humble servants of our Lord Jesus Christ, and we forever mandate that all male and female knights shall be co–equal in this Grand Priory, and that no office, title, or rank shall ever be debarred a Knight Templar on the basis of sex, ethnicity, social or financial status, or Christian tradition.

OSMTJ KNIGHTS TEMPLAR OF AMERICA

Article XV

We will remember the brave and valorous Knights Templar who were martyred in the name of our Lord, and who were unjustly imprisoned, tortured, and burned at the stake on the orders of an Unchristian King.

Article XVI

Membership in the OSMTJ Grand Priory of America conveys no social titles such as "Sir." Instead Christian men who join the organisation are termed "Knights" with the honorific title of Chevalier and females are termed "Dames" with the honorific title of Chevaleresse (or Chevalière).

Article XVII

The OSMTJ Grand Priory of America will forever hold sacred the five indefeasible rules of our Grand Priory:

1). The Temple and Service thereof, for we are the spiritual descendants of the original Nine Knights of the Order, who first held their conclaves in the Holy Temple in Jerusalem, and we look forward to its rebuilding;

2). The Love of Meditation, for we must continually look into our own souls, and ask ourselves if we are truly following in the footsteps of the Master;

3). Discipline, for the principles laid down for the Grand Priory by our patron saint, Bernard of Clairvaux, are still valid today, and we must remember that we are standard bearers for our faith, and never forget that in all personal choices we set an example, whether good or bad;

4). Knightly Combat, for the Blood Red Cross that we wear reminds us that sacrifices are often required of the faithful, and we must always be willing to battle the forces of evil in the spiritual realm. Today's Templars are faced with a spiritual battle instead of a physical one.

5). Brotherhood and Sisterhood, in that each day we must help our brethren, for one day our Lord shall ask us, "Where is thy brother and thy sister?"; and on that day we shall have to give account of ourselves. We must not accept reward, but always be pillars of the Temple, for all the Grand Priory holds for us is the opportunity to flee the sins of the world, to live charitably, to be penitent, and above all, to be the humble servant of Almighty God.

In this, our Holy mandate, to further the aims of Christianity and our Grand Priory, and in particular to enable the Holy Christian Church to carry out the Great Commission, we pledge our lives, our souls, and our knightly honor.

We, the undersigned members of the Ordre Souverain et Militaire du Temple de Jérusalem, representing all the priories in the Confederation, hold that this indefeasible Declaration will henceforth serve as the guiding principles of our Grand Priory, and we declare that any Templars, priories, or governing bodies that depart from them have forfeited their knighthoods and right to be known or called members of the Ordre Souverain et Militaire du Temple de Jérusalem. Let those who violate these principles and bring dishonor to this Grand Priory be summarily expelled, but let those who hold these principles dear and who wish to glorify our Lord be forever known as faithful Knights Templar, and may our Lord give them strength and courage to endure to the end.

Therefore we, the OSMTJ Grand Priory of America, dedicate this Declaration to our most holy Lord Jesus Christ, to whom all hearts are open, all desires known, and no secrets hidden. We hereby submit ourselves to our Lord, and pray that He will cleanse the thoughts of our hearts by the inspiration of His Holy Spirit, that we may perfectly love and faithfully serve Him, and worthily magnify His greatness and holiness, in the name of the Father, the Son, and the Holy Ghost.

We also pray that we, the OSMTJ Grand Priory of America, may find our inheritance in the Kingdom of God with all the holy knights and saints who have found favor with our Lord in ages past.

O God, the protector of all who trust in You, without Whom nothing is strong, nothing is noble, nothing is holy: Increase and multiply upon us Your mercy; that, with You as our Ruler and Guide, we may so pass through things temporal; that we lose not the things eternal; that we be Knights Templar worthy of our charges and oaths, and that we fearlessly battle evil in the spiritual realm; through Jesus Christ our Lord, who lives and reigns with you and the Holy Spirit, one God, forever and ever.

Through Christ, and with Christ, and in Christ, all honor and glory are yours, Almighty God and Father, in the unity of the Holy Spirit, forever and ever. Amen.

Oaths

Knightly Decalogue
Ten Commandments of Knighthood, Leon Gautier, 1832–97

1. The Knight was first of all a Christian soldier with unswerving faith in the Church;
2. He must resolutely defend that Church;
3. He must faithfully obey his feudal lord so long as that obedience did not conflict with allegiance to the Church;
4. He must love his country;
5. He must maintain unrelenting war against the enemies of Christendom;
6. He must never retreat from the enemy;
7. He must keep his pledged word;
8. He must be generous in giving;
9. He must show pity for the weak, and steadfastness in their defence;
10. He must at all times champion the good against the forces of evil.

1813 Templar Oath

"In the name of the Father, of the Son, and of the Holy Ghost."

"I pledge myself, from now and forever, to the holy Militia of the Order of the Temple. I declare to take freely and solemnly oath of obedience, poverty and chastity, as well as fraternity, hospitality and preliation."

"With this oath I state my strong and irrevocable intent"

"To pledge my sword, my forces, my life and everything that I own to the cause, defense, honor and further knowledge of the Christian religion, of the Order of the Temple and of my companions in arms; to the rescue of the Temple of the Holy Sepulchre of our Lord Jesus Christ, of the Land of Palestine and the East and of the domains of our forefathers."

"To submit to the Rule of our Holy Father Bernard, to the Transmission Chart, the Rules, Law and Decrees and all other statements issued in conformity to the Statutes of the Order; not to invest any knight or divulgate title, grade, ritual or other custom of the Order unless authorized by the Statutes; to obey unconditionally and always, within the Establishments of the Order and without, and in all walks of life, the Grand Master and the high Officers of the Order, collectively and singularly."

"To love my brothers the Knight and my Sisters the Dames and help them, their children and their widows with my sword, my advice, means and wealth, my credit and everything in my power, and will favour them, with no exception, over those who are not members of the Order."

"To defend the pious pilgrims, to aid and comfort those who are persecuted for the Cause of the Cross, the sick and the poor."

"To fight the infidels and the non–believers with my example, virtue, charity and convincing arguments; and to fight with the sword the infidels and non–believers who attack the Cross with their own sword."

"To abhor all immodesty, and not to indulge in illegitimate pleasures of the flesh and then only with my legitimate spouse."

"Finally, barring rules dictated by Religion and the Order, to conform to the Laws and Customs of the countries in which I may reside, to fulfill my duties of citizen, and to be loyal knight in those countries which entertain relations with the Order."

"This oath I pronounce loudly before the Knights present at this Convent. I sign it and confirm it by my blood. Again, I write it and sign its registration in the documents relating to this Convent and witnessed by the Knights."

"Glory be to the Father, and to the Son, and to the Holy Ghost. Amen."

"Pursuant to the Magisterial Decrees of 18 Adar 117 and 694, confirmed by the Convent General on 1 Nisan 695 (2 April 1813), I declare to accede to the Unity of the Temple."

The 24 Virtues of a Templar Knight

- **GODLINESS** – Imitating God in your everyday life. Fleeing sin and pursuing righteousness.

- **FAITH** – Trusting in God and His purpose. Seeking God with all your heart knowing that He is always there for you.

- **HOPE** – Knowing that God will provide for our needs if we hope in Him to make the answers in life clear to us.

- **LOVE** – A state of kindness, compassion, humility, patience and intense caring for one another.

- **JUSTICE** – To act justly by doing what is right and pleasing to God. Being fair and square with others.

- **PRUDENCE** – The ability to govern and discipline oneself by the use of reason – making good decisions.

- **TEMPERANCE** – To be moderate with actions, thoughts and deeds. To exhibit restraint and avoid excess.

- **STRENGTH** – The spirit and conviction to live a life that is true to God based on His divine and sanctifying grace.

- **HUMILITY** – To humble ourselves and yield completely to the hand of God being free of pride and arrogance.

- **PERSEVERANCE** – To be patient and committed to pursue something until it has been completed.

- **HONOR** – To serve and live only for God with the highest of respect and esteem – through your actions.

- **CHARITY** – Unlimited kindness and love toward all others.

Giving of your time, talent and treasures.

• **SACRIFICE** – To deny oneself by relinquishing something to the favor of God.

• **COMPASSION** – The feeling of sympathy and sorrow for the unfortunate with a strong desire to alleviate suffering.

• **LOYALTY** – Faithful dedication and loyalty to God with an unwavering commitment.

• **TRUTH** – The honest acceptance of fact and being sincere and candid with others regarding those truths.

• **PURITY** – To be free from anything that taints or impairs goodness. To be free from life–impairing sin.

• **GALLANTRY** – Unbridled courage and bravery knowing that God has provided everything needed to be successful.

• **HOSPITALITY** – Ignoring convenience and going out of your way to help and serve others.

• **COURTESY** – Behavior that is gentle, polite, well–mannered and considerate of others.

• **GRATITUDE** – Being grateful and thankful for all the blessings in life that are gifts from God.

• **GRACE & MERCY** – The humble acceptance and giving of something that is either undeserved or rightly deserved.

• **MENTORSHIP** – Providing wise and influential counsel to others through the exchange of ideas and advice.

• **OVERCOMING FAILURE** – Perseverance over difficult and challenging aspects of life.

Elected Succession of Grand Masters

Founding

1118–1136 Hugues de Payens

1136–1149 Robert de Craon

1149–1152 Everard des Barres

1152–1153 Bernard de Tremalai

1153–1156 Andrew de Montbard

1156–1169 Bertrand de Blanchefort

1169–1171 Philip de Naplous

1171–1179 Odon de St. Amand

1180–1184 Amaud de Toroge

1185–1189 Gerard de Ridefort

1191–1193 Robert de Sable

1194–1200 Gilbert Erail

1201–1209 Philippe de le Plessis

1210–1219 Guillaume de Chartres

1219–1232 Pierre de Montaigue

1232–1244 Armand de Perigord

1244–1247 Richard de Bures

1247–1250 Guillaume de Sonnac

1250–1256 Renaud de Vichiers

1256–1273 Thomas Berard

1273–1291 Guillaume de Beaujeau

1291–1293 Thibaud Gaudin

1294–1314 Jacques de Molay

Restoration of the Ordre du Temple

1681 Jacques Henri de Durfort, Duc de Duras

1705 Philippe II, duc d'Orleans
1724 Louis Augustus Bourbon
1737 Louis Henri Bourbon Conde
1741 Louis-Francois Bourbon Conti
1776 Louis-Hercule Timoleon, Duc de Cosse Brissac
1792 Claude-Mathieu Radix de Chavillon

1804 Bernard Raymond Fabre-Palaprat
1813 Charles Antoine Gabriel, duc de Choiseul
     Charles Louis de Peletier, comte d'Aunay
1827 Bernard Raymond Fabre-Palaprat
1838 William Sidney Smith
1840 Jean-Marie Raoul
1850 Narcisse Valleray (Regent)
1866 Dr. A.G.M. Vernois (Regent)
1892 Joséphin Péladan (Regent)
1894 Secretariat International des Templiers (OSMTH)
1932 Conseil de Regence – Joseph Vandenberg
1935 Theodore Covias (Regent)
1935 Emile-Clement Joseph Isaac Vandenberg (Regent)
1942 Dom Antonio de Sousa Fontes (Regent)
1960 Fernando de Sousa Fontes (Regent)

Ordre Souverain et Militaire du Temple de Jérusalem (OSMTJ)
1970 General Antoine Zdrowjewski
1989 Georges Lamirand
1994 Dr. Nicolas Haimovici Hastier (Regent)

2020

Present Day, His S.E., Master of the Order, General Ronald Mangum

The Knights Templar: A History

Small beginnings, 1095–

In 1095 when Pope Urban II issued the call for the First Crusade, the Western Christian World saw this as a defensive action. Since the early 8th century, Europe had been under ceaseless attacks from Islamic forces beginning with the Iberian Peninsula. Not only was most of Christian Spain conquered, but Islamic armies penetrated into the heart of France, only to be halted by Charles Martel in 732. Still, Islamic forces continued to threaten Europe, occupying Sicily, most of Southern Italy, and even besieging Rome in 846 and sacking St. Peter's Basilica. Yet the First Crusade was not directed at Islam itself, but against the Seljuk Turks, who in their conquest of Palestine replaced the previous Arab tolerance of Christian pilgrims with intolerance and violence. By the end of July 1099, the First Crusade had achieved its objective of restoring the Holy Places to Christian control.

It was one thing to conquer; now the challenge was to rule. Immediately two problems confronted the newly created Kingdom of Jerusalem, being one of the worst examples of feudal fragmentation. The vassals of the King of Jerusalem were carving out their own feudal estates and becoming more powerful than their feudal lord. They were even engaging in conflict among themselves, often hindering efforts to counter any renewed threat from Islam. The second problem was the lack of a reliable fighting force to defend the conquest. Once the Crusade was finished, most of the surviving crusaders, having fulfilled their vows, returned home. The Knights Templar would provide the solution by becoming the first international standing army.

The opportunity came in 1118–19, when an idealistic band of knights led by Hugues de Payens offered their services to protect pilgrims en route to the Holy Places. Organizing themselves into a religious community, vows were made to the Latin Patriarch of Jerusalem. Baldwin II, King of Jerusalem, provided them with quarters in what had been the al–Aqsa Mosque, thought to be part of Solomon's Temple. They became known as the Poor Knights of Christ of the Temple of Solomon, or simply the Knights of the Temple. Perhaps it was the King, who saw in these Poor Knights of Christ, the opportunity to create a fighting force. This was reinforced when the counts of Anjou and Champaigne joined the Order.

Now events moved to Europe. If this humble group of knights was to become an effective military force, papal recognition, autonomy, and an economic foundation had to be acquired. Hugues de Payens himself went to Europe on a mission to gain support and recruit new members. More importantly, the support of the outstanding church leader of the period was enlisted, Bernard, the Cistercian abbot of Clairvaux. In 1128–29 a Council was held at Troyes in Champaigne in which The Order of the Temple was recognized and provided with a Rule, drafted under Bernard's guidance. Pope Honorius II approved the recognition, with Hugues de Payens becoming the first Master of the Temple.

It was Bernard de Clairvaux, who grasped the historical significance, when he wrote in Delaude Novae Militae (In Praise of a New Knighthood) that a new type of Order had been created, consisting of laymen who blended the knightly and monastic life. These soldier–monks would fight to protect Christian interests. While Hugues de Payens had been the leader with a mission and a vision, an individual possessed of administrative talent was needed. That was Robert de Craon, who became Master of the Temple c 1136.

By the time of the death of Grand Master de Craon in 1149, a series of popes had granted privileges that made the Templars an autonomous corporate body, answerable only to the papacy. Papal and royal exemptions allowed the Templars to become economically independent, financing their overseas military endeavors in great part from European donations of land and money. In the process, the Templars fashioned the first European–wide system of international banking. Their convents, particularly in London and Paris, became "clearing–houses" for the deposit, disbursement and transfer of funds. The system's reliability for efficiency and honesty attracted church leaders and kings to entrust their funds and valuables to Templar security.

Their independence allowed the Templars to create an effective fighting force, a naval fleet, and a defensive system of fortresses in Palestine/Syria. Within the Iberian Peninsula, Templars supported the Reconquista, led by the Spanish and Portuguese kings. At the height of their power in the 13th century, the Order had around 7,000 members, including knights, sergeants–at–arms, non–military–sergeants, brothers, and priests. Their network consisted of some 870 castles, preceptories and convents spread throughout most of Christian Europe, Palestine and Syria. They inspired both the Hospitallers and the Teutonic Knights to adopt military roles. The Templars served as a model for new military orders established by the rulers within the Iberian Peninsula, such as Calatrava in Castile and Santiago in Leon.

In 1146, Pope Eugenius III granted the Templars the privilege of wearing the Red Cross or Cross Patteé on their mantles as a symbol of their willingness to shed their blood. Noted for their bravery, determination and discipline, much of the burden for the defense of the Crusader States fell upon them. Described as "lions in battle," thousands of Templars gave their lives as they won everlasting glory in such battles as Cresson, Hattin, La Forbie and Mansurah. Despite their efforts, Jerusalem was lost to Saladin in 1187. The Templars established themselves at Acre, following the limited success of the Third Crusade. After the loss of Acre in 1291, the Templars, evacuating their last castles in Palestine/Syria, retreated to the island of Cyprus.

Who Was to Blame? 1200–

Who was responsible for the loss of the Crusader States? The Templars may have shared in the blame, due to ineffectual leadership and involvement in politics. But there were more important reasons, such as the failure to establish an effective political order in Palestine and the tendency of the great lords to become embroiled in political intrigue instead of defending the Kingdom against the common enemy. The arrival of new crusaders insisting upon pursuing the Holy War often upset the balance of power that had been achieved between the Christians and Muslims, thus encouraging a strong Islamic reaction. The problem of leadership was never solved. Even the kings made poor leaders of the Crusades, since their political distrust followed them to Palestine and they, too, had to return to their home kingdoms.

The idealism and moral inspiration of the First Crusade became tarnished and corrupted by greed for political power and wealth. Finally, there was the Islamic reaction that found effective leaders, such as Saladin, to lead the counter–attack to the European presence in the Middle East. In short, the odds were not only against the survival of the Crusader States but against the Templars as an enduring fighting force in the Middle East.

By the late 13th century, questions were being raised about the effectiveness of the military orders with proposals being made to unify them. The fall of Acre made the issue more pressing. While both the Hospitallers and the Teutonic Knights found new roles for themselves, the Templars lacked economic resources that were essential for any renewal of their military prowess due to the loss of lands in Palestine and Syria, the decline from patrons of gifts of land and money, the curtailing of their exemptions, and the impact of inflation. Recruitment became more difficult as the Templars became an aging Order. Moreover, the appearance of possessing great wealth became the kiss of death. Rulers, motivated by greed and jealousy, took advantage of the Templars' loss of credibility and respect. Already in the early 14th century, English kings had violated the temple of the Templars in London.

Ultimately the fate of the Templars would be decided within France. Phillip IV, King of France, made the move to challenge the continued existence of the Templars. Taking advantage of rumors of Templar corruption (no doubt exaggerated) and of a weak and compliant Pope, in 1307, Phillip IV ordered the arrest of all Templars in France, including the Master of the Temple, Jacques de Molay. Pope Clement V ordered an investigation into the charges leveled against the Templars. Under immense political pressure, the Pope ordered the arrest of all Templars within Christian Europe and the seizure of their property.

In an attempt to resolve the Templar issue, Clement V convoked the Council of Vienne in 1312. The lack of credible incriminating evidence led the majority of the council fathers to conclude that the charges lacked merit. Then the Pope on his own authority issued the Bull, Vox in excelso, dissolving the Order. Templars were to be pensioned off and their property turned over to the Hospitallers.

The final act came on March 18, 1314, when Phillip IV ordered the execution by fire of Jacques de Molay and Geoffroy de Charnay as relapsed heretics. Finding courage at the end, they both vigorously denied the charges against the Order. In 1312, after the Council of Vienne, and under extreme pressure from King Phillip IV, Pope Clement V issued an edict claiming to dissolve the Order. But since the Order had existed eleven years before Papal recognition (founded in 1118, recognized by the Pope in 1129 at the Council of Troyes), the Pope only had the power to remove his ecclesiastical recognition.

Many kings and nobles, who had been supporting the Knights up until that time, finally acquiesced and dissolved the orders in their fiefs in accordance with the Papal command. Most were not as brutal as the French. In England, many Knights were arrested and tried, but not found guilty. Much of the Templar property outside of France was transferred by the Pope to the Knights Hospitaller, and many surviving Templars were also accepted into the Hospitallers.

In the Iberian Peninsula, where the king of Aragon was against giving the heritage of the Templars to Hospitallers (as commanded by Clement V), the Order of Montesa took Templar assets. The order continued to exist in Portugal, simply changing its name to the Order of Christ. This group was believed to have contributed to the first naval discoveries of the Portuguese. For example, Prince Henry the Navigator led the Portuguese order for twenty years until the time of his death. In Scotland, after Templars played a significant role in the Scottish victory at Bannockburn on June 24, 1314, Robert the Bruce joined the Templars and Hospitallers into a new Order of the Temple and of St. John.

Even with the absorption of Templars into other Orders, there are still questions as to what became of all of the tens of thousands of Templars across Europe. There had been 15,000 "Templar Houses", and an entire fleet of ships. Even in France where hundreds of Templars had been rounded up and arrested, this was only a small percentage of the estimated 3,000 Templars in the entire country. Also, the extensive archive of the Templars, with detailed records of all of their business holdings and financial transactions, was never found. By papal bull it was to have been transferred to the Hospitallers, whose library was destroyed in the 16th century by Turkish invaders.

Some scholars believe that a number of Templars fled into the Swiss Alps. There are records of Swiss villagers around that time suddenly becoming very skilled military tacticians. An attack was led by Leopold I of Austria, who was attempting to take control of the St.

Gotthard Pass with a force of 5,000 knights. His force was ambushed and destroyed by a group of about 1,500 Swiss peasants. Up until that point, the Swiss really had no military experience, but after that battle, the Swiss became renowned as seasoned fighters. Some folk tales from the period describe how there were "armed white knights" who came to help them in their battles. This may have been where the underground Templar "Brotherhood" ended up, in the Cantons (provinces) of Switzerland. It would explain why the Swiss flag is a Templar symbol on a red background. And it would explain why the Swiss suddenly took over where the Templars had left of as the bankers of Europe. Templar influence seems to be reflected in the coats of arms used by the Swiss Cantons and even in the naming of some Swiss locations like the Town of Sion.

Restoration of the Order, 1705–

Did the Templars survive as an underground order after 1314? We will probably never know. In any case, the restored Order came into public view in Versailles, France, in 1705. It was at that time that a Convent General of the Order elected Philippe, Duke of Orleans, later Regent of France, to the Grand Mastership of the Order.

In 1736 Andrew Michael Ramsay, a Scottish Freemason and Catholic, delivered a speech to the Masonic Lodge in Paris, insisting that Freemasonry had begun in Palestine among the crusades, particularly the military orders. The result was a frenzy of new rituals, symbols, and myths based on the Crusades and the military orders. When the battle of Culloden in 1746 ended any hope of a Stuart restoration, French Freemasonry began to develop its own identity. Now a German noble and Freemason, the Baron Karl von Hund, revealed his belief that he had discovered a new form of Freemasonry, known as the Strict Observance, directly descendant from the Templars. It was based on Templar survival in the British Isles, particularly in Scotland. This belief in Templar survival became very popular among various Masonic lodges. Meanwhile, continental lodges were being influenced by the rationalism of the Enlightenment with many members becoming supporters of revolutionary change directed against absolute monarchy and a social order based on birth and privilege. Then came the French Revolution in 1789, with its promise of a New Order founded on brotherhood, equality and liberty. Out of the turmoil created by the Revolution, a "child of the Revolution", Napoleon Bonaparte, rose to power, promising to spread the ideals of the Revolution to all of Europe. After conquering most of continental Europe, he had himself proclaimed Emperor. In that same year of 1804, the restored Ordre du Temple (Order of the Temple) was founded by Dr. Fabre–Palaprat, a chiropodist, Ledru, a medical Doctor, Claude–Mathieu, and Radix de Chevillon. Fabre–Palaprat accepted the office of Grand Master.

Under the leadership of Dr. Bernard Raymond Fabre'–Palaprat, the Order began to flourish again, especially with the patronage of Napoleon Bonaparte. Fabre'–Palaprat was a product of the Age of Enlightenment, and saw Templarism as an expression of help, decency, dedication and chivalrous behavior. He had a remarkable talent for communicating the romantic ideals of knighthood to other people and, as a result, many prominent citizens became members and the Order grew rapidly. At the same time, two interesting documents surfaced. One was the Charter of Transmission, by which an alleged successor to de Molay, Jean M. Larmenius, provided for the secret survival of the Knights Templar. This document, written in ciphers, also included in cipher the signatures of Grand Masters from Larmenius to Fabre–Palaprat. The second document was the Statutes of 1705, written under the direction of Philip, the Duke of Orleans, whom the founders of 1804 claimed as a restorer of the Templars.

For motives of his own, Napoleon Bonaparte approved of this "restoration", even allowing a grand ceremony in Paris, honoring de

Molay and all other Templar martyrs. Napoleon, upon becoming Emperor, created a new nobility. Perhaps he saw these new Templars as serving as a counter–balance to the Masonic lodges, whom he distrusted due to their political radicalism.

By 1808, through successful recruitment the new Order had established Priories and Commanderies throughout most of the Grand Empire, including Italy and Switzerland. Ties to its Masonic origins were severed, with this Order of the Temple proclaiming its autonomy and adherence to "the Catholic Apostolic and Roman religion." This promising beginning was quickly dashed by Fabre–Palaprat when he revised the Statutes of 1705 to justify assuming absolute power, a schism erupted that lasted until 1814.

When unity was finally restored, the Order once again prospered. When constitutional monarchy was established in France, the Order supported the restored Bourbon King, Louis XVIII, and the king in return granted the Templars recognition. When Charles X attempted to restore royal absolutism, the Templars supported the revolt of 1830 and the return of constitutional monarchy. Once again Fabre–Palaprat became the source of contention. Earlier he had formed the Johannite Church of the Primitive Christians. When, in 1833, he attempted to impose his Johannite beliefs upon the Templars, the result was once more schism. One faction retained its chivalric traditions and obedience to the Catholic Church. The death of Fabre–Palaprat in 1838 provided another opportunity for unity. This attempt failed when the French Palaprien Templars refused to accept the choice of Sir William Sidney–Smith, the British Grand Prior, as Grand Master. A bright period for the Order of the Temple occurred in 1853, when, by royal decree, Emperor Napoleon III recognized the Ordre du Temple ("Palaprien," those that followed in the line of Palaprat) with the right to wear its insignia and decorations within France. Inside France, the Palaprien Templars continued to choose Regents until the defeat and capture of Napoleon III by the Prussians in 1870, causing the Ordre du

Temple to lose it's strongest protector. The centrally organized Palaprien Templars soon faded from existence except that several of their former priories continued on autonomously.

The Years of the Regents (Caretakers), 1930–

The Templar revival in the 20th century owed its existence to developments within the Grand Priory of Belgium, which had been founded under Dr. Fabre–Palaprat in 1825. Factional disputes between Catholic and Masonic members, along with European political developments, resulted in its being put to sleep for several years. In 1932, several former members re–established the Belgian Grand Priory, taking the name of "The Sovereign and Military Order of the Temple of Jerusalem." Hoping to re–establish this Order of the Temple as an international organization, a Regency was formed. The idea behind this Regency was that it would function as the temporary leadership of the Order until a new Grand Master could be elected.

Emile Isaac, who later took on his wife's last name, "Vandenberg," to hide his Jewish ancestry from the Nazis, was a key figure at this time. As Regent of this Belgian Grand Priory, Emile devoted much of his energy to revitalizing Templar Priories across Europe, including France, Italy, Portugal and Switzerland. Such a promising development was cut short by the Second World War. Viewing the German occupation of Belgium as a danger to Templar survival, Vandenberg made a temporary transfer of the leadership and archives of the Order to the care of the Portuguese Grand Prior, Antonio Campello de Sousa Fontes. Later in 1943, Emile requested the return of the archives. Then, de Sousa Fontes took advantage of the sudden death of Emile in that same year to assume the title of Regent. Once more there was schism, with some Priories rejecting his leadership. Sadly, there is evidence that the "car accident" that killed Emile Isaac was orchestrated by the Nazis who wanted this high–profile Jewish Templar dead13.

In 1960 Antonio Campello de Sousa Fontes passed away and left it in his will that his son should succeed him as Regent of the order. It is interesting to note that the original Last Will and Testament of Antonio de Sousa Fontes was dated August 20, 1948, and not certified by a notary with the amended changes designating his son as successor until February 26, 1960, which was eleven days after Antonio de Sousa Fontes had already passed away! How a deceased man could have amended his will to provide for the succession of his son is a mystery we'll never be able to solve. Thus, in 1960, when Fernando Campello de Sousa Fontes tried to succeed his father, ascribing to himself the title of Prince Regent, he met stiff resistance. Since the beginning of the Order in 1118, Grand Masters had always been elected and hereditary succession of the Grand Master's seat has no precedence. Therefore many of the priories did not accept de Sousa Fontes's son as the legitimate leader of the order and they soon got tired of the despotic way he tried to rule the Order.

In 1969, Regent de Sousa Fontes issued a Magistral Edict convoking an International Convent General that would first meet in Paris in September, 1970, with the purpose of electing a new Grand Master. Many of the Priories were tired of de Sousa Fontes's despotic and undemocratic leadership, his utter contempt for transparency, and blatant mismanagement. At that historic Convent General in Paris, participants democratically elected General Antoine (originally Andrzej) Zdrojewski (the Grand Prior of Europe and of France) to be the next Grand Master. It's important to note that de Sousa Fontes authorized and attended this Paris Convent for the purpose of electing a new Grand Master as he believed he was going to win. In anticipation, Fontes had even prearranged a symbolic "victory lap" of two additional Conclaves: the first scheduled for 1971 in Chicago, Illinois, and the last in 1973 in Portugal.

Zdrojewski had been the Chief of the Polish Military Operations in France. The relationship between the French and Poles, fighting a common enemy, was very friendly. The Polish Government in Exile was also covertly regrouping remnants of army units (what would have been the 3rd and 4th Polish Infantry Divisions) for direct military contact to destabilize the German occupation of France. General Juliusz Kleeberg mustered one of the largest secret armies in France. The unit became known as the Polish Organization for Fighting for Independence (POWN) and was later commanded by Colonel Zdrojewski. Zdrojewski became a war hero by distinguishing himself as the commander of this secret army and in 1944, after becoming a French citizen, the French Government promoted Zdrojewski to General.9 6 1

The defeated Fontes was both shocked and furious upon the election of Zdrojewski but he wasn't willing to obey the Templar Rule of Succession by giving up power. He tried to have the results nullified by saying that General Zdrojewski was only elected Grand Master because the French Grand Priory had been "infiltrated" by the Gualist Secret Police, Service d'Action Civique (S.A.C.). Similar to the CIA or MI6 of today, the S.A.C. was established by President Charles de Gaulle as a 1901 law association on January 4th, 1960, in the proclaimed aim of providing unconditional support to de Gaulle's policies.2 While it was true that the French Grand Priory included members from the S.A.C., it was certainly not "infiltrated." Rather, these were their legitimately accepted members. General Zdrojewski had served under, been promoted to General by, and fully supported his former Commander, President Charles de Gaulle. He knew full well who the S.A.C. members were and accepted them into his French Grand Priory.

History is written by the political powers that survive to tell the tale. While President Charles de Gaulle was in power, the S.A.C. were the heroes defending the Republic and protecting President Charles de Gaulle during the precarious years following World War II. But when de Gaulle's political enemies took power, they portrayed the S.A.C. as criminals (dirt can be found on even the best of organizations). Saying that the French Grand Priory was "infiltrated" by the S.A.C. is as ridiculous as saying the Templars of today have been infiltrated by retired military personnel. The Templars of today are fully aware that much of their ranks consist of retired military personnel and welcome them in.

Fontes's failed attempt to have the election results nullified caused a split in the OSMTH. Some of the Grand Priories, including the French, Belgian, Swiss, and Polish, followed the newly elected General Zdrojewski, and some stayed with the defeated Fontes. Alfred Zappelli (Grand Prior of Switzerland), General Georges de Bruyn (Grand Prior of Belgium), and Badouraly–Somji Alibay (Commander of the Polish Commandery) were also backers of General Zdrojewski. After the election of Zdrojewski, our branch became known as OSMTJ (or "OSMTJ–Zdrojewski"). Those who continued to follow de Sousa Fontes were known as OSMTH (or "OSMTH–Regency"). "OSMTJ" is the French acronym for, "Ordre Souverain et Militaire du Temple de Jérusalem." "OSMTH" is the latin translation of that: "Ordo Supremus Militaris Templi Hierosolymitani" ("Hierosolymitani" means "Jerusalem"). In English, you could translate the latin to, the "Supreme (or Sovereign) Military Order of the Temple of Jerusalem."

On February 22, 1971, Grand Master Zdrojewski convened a Grand Council meeting of all member Grand Priories in Paris at Richelieu I. The first motion passed at this Grand Council was a decree that Fernando de Sousa Fontes was henceforth, stripped of all titles, ranks, and had lost his right to wear the robes and insignia of the Order. The reason for this was that the aforementioned had displayed no respect for the hierarchy or rules of succession of the Order and had committed violations of the rules of discipline of the Order. Specifically, Fernando de Sousa Fontes was known to sell ranks and titles in the order without merit. In fact, although the rules of the Order set forth only one Grand Prior per country at a time, Fernando de Sousa Fontes had accepted bribes to appoint several concurrent Grand Priors in many countries ("Grand Prior" is supposed to be the title for the one national leader in each country). For example, Fontes has accepted bribes to appoint six simultaneous Grand Priors in France, five in Spain, two in the United States twice (simultaneous U.S. Grand Priories in '64 & again in '95), two in Scotland, and two in Serbia. Each of these Grand Priors, being lead to believe they would be the only leader of their nation, had to pay a small fortune to de Sousa Fontes for that position only to discover Fontes was reselling that position to others!

In late 1973, Grand Master Zdrojewski carried out a reorganization of the OSMTJ and a reform of the Statutes. He approved the Grand Priories re-asserting the independence of the International Federation of Autonomous Grand Priories of the OSMTJ (Each member Grand Priory was recognized as autonomous). The Swiss Grand Priory accepted these reformed statutes in 1973 while the Belgian and United States Grand Priories accepted them in 1975.

One of the OSMTJ's most important leaders at this time was the Grand Prior of Switzerland, Alfred Zappelli. Zappelli moved to Geneva where he was a Banker and Financial Consultant.3 He became the Grand Prior of Switzerland from 1967 until the mid 90's except for a brief falling out with the Grand Master resulting in his expulsion in 1971 and reinstatement the following year. The OSMTJ suffered some tumultuous years from 1974, until near the end of the 70's when it was necessary for Grand Master Zdrojewski to keep a low profile due to changes in the political powers of France (the election of new French President Valéry Giscard d'Estaing in 1974). Certain repercussions were meted out in the form of "investigations" (witch–hunts) on high profile supporters of former French President Charles de Gaulle and on former members of the S.A.C.. General Zdrojewski had been one of de Gaulle's staunchest supporters. During these years, Grand Prior Alfred Zappelli stepped up to hold the OSMTJ together. Zappelli recruited and introduced Philip A. Guarino to Grand Master Zdrojewski who appointed Philip the Grand Prior of the United States on February 15th, 1973. Zappelli went on to found several other Grand Priories including one in Italy under Pasquale Gugliotta, who was named Grand Bailli of Italy on June 16, 1976. Zappelli continued giving lectures about the Knights Templar and recruiting for the OSMTJ all over the world. Despite his important position, Zappelli was a humble man and the Grand Priory he established still exists today.

General Antoine Zdrojewski remained Grand Master until his death in 1989. Before his death, in 1986, he issued a Charter of Transmission that gave authority to Georges Lamirand, the Grand Seneschal, and nominated him as his successor. Lamirand, the Director of the Billancourt Renault factory, had been serving as the Grand Prior of France. As Zdrojewski had wished, Georges Lamirand succeed Zdrowjewski as Regent (Caretaker) of the order, and then he went on to be elected Grand Master. Lamirand had started the war as an Artillery Officer in 1939, but had been promoted quickly through the ranks to become the Vichy General Secretary of Youth from September 1940 to March 1943. Starting in 1943, he covertly started working for the French Resistance and after '43, he openly worked against the Vichy Government. Lamirand was also the Mayor of La Bourbole, Puy de Dome from 1955–1971. In the last decade of his life, Georges Lamirand was in poor health and appointed Dr. Nicolas Haimovici Hastier to the office of Grand Commander and Guardian of the Faith.11

When Lamirand died on February 5th, 1994, his Grand Commander and Guardian of the Faith, Dr. Nicolas Haimovici Hastier, became the Regent of the Order. Dr. Nicolas was a naturalized French citizen, married to a German, and had lived a long time in Nice, France (on the French Riviera) before moving to Sanremo, Italy.11

Nicolas was a distinguished physician with more than 100

published scientific articles in peer–reviewed medical journals, as well as a consultant to the American Administration (Served in a Medical Overseeing capacity on several Navy ships including The USS Enterprise). He taught in various universities in France and for 12 years he taught at New York Medical College (Paramus, New Jersey) He was a District Governor of Rotary in France and an officer in many other humanitarian organizations. Nicolas was a brilliant Author and in 2001 he wrote the book, The Rule of the Order of the Templars. It took him about 15 years to write this book and is considered his masterpiece. Regent Nicolas promoted General Ronald Mangum to Deputy Regent in March of 2018.

On January 2, 2020, the Grand Priors of the Order called an election, finally ending the Regency of Dr. Hastier, and elected our new Grand Master, His S.E., Master of the Order, General Ronald Mangum.

Of those Priories that had initially stayed faithful to de Sousa Fontes following his 1970 defeat, it didn't take long for the majority to realize that they had stayed with the wrong man. Fernando De Sousa Fontes, up until this time, had called himself the "Regent" or caretaker of the order until such a time that a Grand Master could be elected. Now he changed his tune as he continued dismantling every democratic process in the OSMTH until he unilaterally changed the statutes to give himself the title of "Grand Master." His revised statutes, which he created in 1990, stated that if a Grand Master had not been elected for 903 days, the Regent automatically becomes Grand Master for life without an election! When his national leaders united in their request for a Council of Grand Priors to allow them to have some input, Fontes mocked them by creating this council with only his family as members! In 1995 a lawsuit was filed against Fontes and there were allegations of him having misspent a significant portion of membership dues to fund his own lavish lifestyle.7

At this point, in November of 1995, the majority of the OSMTH Grand Priories under Fontes assembled in the Austrian town of Salzburg and democratically voted to leave Fernando de Sousa Fontes, in effect, creating a new OSMTH Order (the original Order under Fontes being called the "OSMTH–Regency or OSMTH–Porto"). It's important to note that their Grand Master, de Sousa Fontes, neither authorized nor attended this meeting and that no election took place at this meeting.12 We respect this new OSMTH as our Brothers and Sisters for we understand why they broke away from de Sousa Fontes.

Pictorial Guide to the History of the Order:

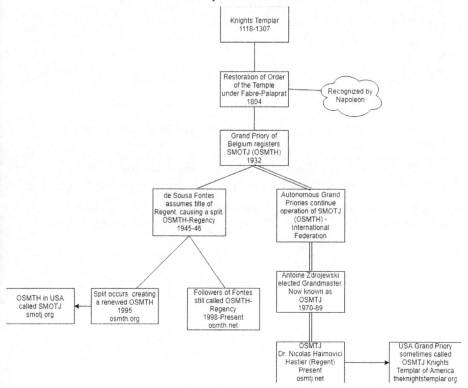

References

(1) Zdrojewski promoted to General:
http://www.swordforum.com/forums/showthread.php?75540–Would–love–some–assistance–on–this–sword

(2) SAC (French: *Service d'Action Civique*; or *Civic Action Service*
https://en.wikipedia.org/wiki/Service_d'Action_Civique

(3) Alfred Zappelli http://news.google.com/newspapers?
nid=1291&dat=19771002&id=lidUAAAAIBAJ&sjid=B40DAAAAIBAJ&pg=4825%2C4612611

(4) Pasquale Gugliotta named Bailli of Italy

(6) Background on General Antoine (or Antoni) Zdrojewski about
http://pl.wikipedia.org/wiki/Antoni_Zdrojewski

(7) See Lawsuit: SMOTJ Inc. v. de Sousa Fontes, case No. U.S.D.C. Texas No. 3–995CV–0890G

(8) History of Philip A. Guarino: http://www.TheKnightsTemplar.org/philip–guarino/

(9) History of Zdrojewski in WWII: http://www.PolandInExile.com/exile4.htm

(11) Venceslai, Stelio. L'Utopia Templare. Rome: Laris Editrice, 2011 . Print. Pages: 109–112.

(12) See the history leading up to this meeting and what took place:
http://www.theknightstemplar.org/forums/topic/fontes–versus–smotj–osmth–kti/)

(13) Read the history of Emile Isaac (Vandenberg):
http://mechelen.mapt.be/wiki/Emile_Clement_Joseph_Isaac_Vandenberg

What it Means To Be a Templar Today

By Reverend Timothy Weddell, OSMTJ–USA

Chaplain & Anglican Minister

The original premise of those nine French knights who came to Jerusalem in 1118 A.D was strictly Christian in intent. These Poor Fellow soldiers of Jesus Christ blended the character of the monk with that of the soldier and thus these powerful and devoted military friars became the Delta Force, SAS and SEALS of the medieval period during the Crusades. Protecting pilgrims traveling to Jerusalem and defending the Holy City, they faithfully served God and the Faith for almost 200 years during this period.

To take upon ourselves the name of the Knights Templar in the 21st Century is quite an assumption! In this age of "political correctness" the very idea would be most repulsive to those peaceniks and unrealistic idealists. Such a culture evolved in Jerusalem after the death of King David under the leadership of David's son, King Solomon. We can read about this period in the Book of Solomon's Song 4:4. It reads, *"...the tower of David builded for an armory, whereon there hang a thousand bucklers, all shields of mighty men."*

In less than a generation, because of the exploits of "the mighty men," the ancient nation of Israel had peace. Israel also had something else, lethargy and complacency! These "might men" and their arms had become nothing more than legends and tales. Solomon had made their bucklers and shields museum pieces in the tower. A casual perusal of 1 Chronicles 11:22–23 reveals the character of these mighty men. Benaiah slew two lion–like men of Moab and he slew a lion in a pit on a snowy day! He single–handedly fell upon an Egyptian soldier who stood over seven feet tall, taking the Egyptian's own spear out of his hand with which he killed the seven footer. That spear, most likely was in Solomon's museum.

Of course, this is just one of many illustrations of "The Mighty Men of David." Because of these men, Solomon was barely challenged for forty years. Good thing too, the nation became soft and compromised and shortly after Solomon's death, the Kingdom divided and eventually fell to the enemy.

Our day is much like Solomon's. Compromise abounds, lethargy rules and complacency is the cure! Never in the history of the world has there been a greater need for men and women of integrity and principle! In a world where 1 Christian is killed every 11 minutes, undefined Christianity is no problem for anyone! We have elevated personality above character in every sphere. We seek entertainment in church instead of worship. We embrace tolerance instead of truth. We value success over substance, and we place the need of man over God and His glory.

It was in such a world as ours that the Knights Templar marched with integrity and honor and by the Grace of Almighty God, made a difference. So can we in our day. The current cultural and societal trends must be reversed or Western Culture (which has had an overall positive impact on world culture) will be entirely lost.

The moral of the story is simple: we are not just to be like the Knights Templar of old, we are the KNIGHTS TEMPLAR and we are here to show the world the glory and honor of valor, strength, courage and integrity! We are here to show the world the glorious Red Cross of Jesus Christ! Knights, Arise!

Details of Working in the Modern Order

Today's Order of the Knights Templar takes its inspiration from the highest ideals and values of the medieval Order of the Knights Templar. We are their spiritual heirs.

Our members are committed to vows of Knighthood and to live a life of honor by exhibiting certain virtues. We choose a life of purpose and meaning by taking a stand for what is right in our families, our community and our nation.

The Knights Templar has a rich and powerful history that spans nearly 900 years. Since our beginning in the year 1118 A.D., The Knights Templar has been living a life dedicated to the honor and glory of our Lord, Jesus Christ. Our modern day mission is to help the poor, the sick, the persecuted, the old, the needy, the helpless, the hungry, the cold and the unprotected.

Today, we thrive with an international membership of men and women who are dedicated to living and sharing a life according to the teachings of our Lord and Savior, Jesus Christ. As the saying goes: *You get out what you put in.*

This is true with many things in life and it applies here as well. Active participation in our Order not only honors our Lord, but it will also provide a meaningful reward that comes to you from the fellowship and love common among your Brothers and Sisters in Christ.

To New Companions At Arms:

As a new Companion-at-Arms, you will be assigned a Mentor who will guide you along the way. Your mentor will be there for you to answer any questions or concerns that you may have. You are encouraged to maintain a close relationship with your mentor and seek guidance along your journey.

Becoming active and staying active will enhance your journey to Knighthood and it will also serve as the foundation for our ultimate journey to be with our Lord in Heaven.

Visit your Priory or Commandery Facebook page regularly. Don't hesitate to post about your feelings, experiences and prayers. Take advantage of the postings of others. To broaden and deepen your experience, become friends with others within the Order and take your lead for actions based upon what you learn from them.

Our Order is international, consisting of 34 Grand Priories throughout the world. A Priory is a group of men or women under religious vows headed by a Prior.

These Priories are: Argentina, France, Mexico, Slovenia, Armenia, Germany, Netherlands, Spain, Belgium, Greece, Norway, Suisse, Brazil, Hungary, Peru, Tasmania, Bulgaria, Iceland, Portugal, Ukraine, Canada, Indonesia, Puerto Rico, Venezuela, Costa Rica, Ireland, Romania, United States, Czech Rep., Italy, Scotland, Ecuador, Latvia, and Serbia.

Within the United States, every effort is made to hold a National Conclave every year to gather as many members together as are able.

Structure of OSMTJ and the Grand Priory of America

Your Priory is one of the many parts making up the national body of the US Grand Priory. The US Grand Priory includes all the members in all the priories within the United States and is headed by the Grand Prior and the Executive Council.

A Priory is a subdivision of the Order and it often covers a large area. The leader of a Priory is a Prior (or sometimes a Master

Commander). A Priory can be further subdivided into Commanderies headed by a Knight Commander.

In addition, some priories form smaller units called "Troops" wherever there is a cluster of members in the same area. The Troops can meet as often as they like in person to enjoy fellowship, perform service projects and give mutual support.

Each Priory performs at least one priory–wide, real life event per year. This will usually be the Investiture Service where new knights are given their accolade. If there is no Investiture in that year, a Recognition and Rewards Banquet will be held instead.

Each priory covers a specific region of the United States. Presently, there are 13 Priories and 20 Commanderies that are aligned within those priories. Each priory is autonomous, but they all report to our Grand Seneschal and Grand Prior.

The Grand Priory Church Board (Governing Authority)

Grand Prior – Bryant Jones – Grand Prior is his proper title and he is to be addressed as such.

Grand Seneschal – Caesar Johnson – to be addressed as Grand Seneschal Caesar.

Grand Secretary – Bob Zalner – to be addressed as Grand Secretary.

Grand Marshal – Tim Woods – to be addressed as Grand Marshal.

List of General Officers:

International Grandmaster – His S.E. General Ronald S. Mangum

International Grand Chancellor – Bryant Jones

Grand Prior USA – Bryant Jones

OSMTJ KNIGHTS TEMPLAR OF AMERICA

Grand Seneschal – Caesar Johnson

Grand Secretary – Bob Zalner

Grand Marshal – Tim Woods

Grand Turcopolier – Prior Trey Emery

Grand Chancellor – Rev. Ray Jones

Grand Treasurer – Deacon James McDonough

Grand Almoner – Tony Woodard

Deputy Grand Almoner – Michael Laverne

Grand Communications Officer – Prior Willard Carpenter

Grand Historian/Chronicler – Michael Denton

Deputy Grand Historian – Paul A. Copenhagen

Grand Barrister – Atty. Timothy Whitley

Grand Herald – Keith Menefee

Deputy Grand Secretary – Ken Zalner

Ambassador to Europe – Luis Antonio Colon–Arce

Ambassador to South America – Augusto Leon–Braga

National Sword Bearer – Donald Thompson

National Standard Bearer – Deacon James McDonough

National Video Director – Bruce Kaufman

National Draper – Commander Mark Pica

National Scribe – John Bousquet

Templar Church Ranks

Bishop of Templar Church – Bishop Fitzgerald

National Chaplain – Jim Lanley

Viceroy – Stephen Shutt

Attorney of Templar Church – Atty. Ronald S. Mangum (ret. Army)

Duties of a Companion At Arms

- Spread the light of Christ in an increasingly dark world.

- Practice works of mercy, charity and benevolence.

- Act as a force to unify all Christians under the banner of Christ.

- Perpetuate Knights Templar traditions by defending Christendom.

- Live a life of Chivalry and hold each other accountable for excellence.

- Promote historical studies, heraldry and the genealogy of the Order.

- Promote the values of friendship, loyalty and respect, feelings of universal brotherhood and ideals of solidarity among all people.

Ranks

Rank is something you earn. From Highest to lowest the ranks are:

• PRIOR – The leader of a Priory.

• MASTER COMMANDER – The lowest rank at which a person

can lead a priory

• KNIGHT COMMANDER – The preferred rank for leading a Commandery

• KNIGHT CAPTAIN – The lowest rank a person can lead a Commandery

• KNIGHT LIEUTENANT – The preferred rank at which a person can lead a ministry within the priory.

• KNIGHT – Required rank for ministry leadership position. Receives full accolade of knighthood with cross and mantle.

• SERGEANT MAJOR – Executive Officer of Sergeants Corps

• MASTER SERGEANT – Executive Officer of CAA Corps

• FIRST SERGEANT – The lead Sergeant of other sergeants within a priory.

• STAFF SERGEANT – Preferred rank of a Sergeant who leads or operates a ministry in the priory.

• SERGEANT–AT–ARMS – Entry level rank for person completing Templar Basic Training and no longer on probation. Receives neck cross and certificate.

• COMPANION–AT–ARMS – The entry level rank of members older than 18. It brings full membership, but is also probationary.

• SQUIRE – The child of an existing member at least 14 years old but younger than 18 who wishes to affiliate with the Order. Does not have full membership, but can participate in some activities.

• PAGE – The child of an existing member between the ages of 7 and 13 who wishes to affiliate with the Order. Does not have full membership, but can participate in some activities.

In addition to these basic ranks which are at the local level, there are many additional ranks that can be earned as you progress over time. For a complete summary of those ranks, go to our web site here: http://www.theknightstemplar.org/ranks/

Regarding OFFICER POSITIONS: Officer positions are appointed and based on the skills, talents and abilities of the person. To be considered, a person must be at the rank of Knight or higher and have demonstrated leadership ability.

Rank Etiquette

Whenever possible and known, please address people by their proper title. For example:

• Companions at Arms – All are simply referred to as "brother/sister" and first name, i.e., CAA Jim Smith would be "Brother Jim", CAA Pam Smith would be "Sister Pam".

• Squire / Page – Referred to by that designation and their first name, i.e., Squire Dan Jones would be Squire Dan. Page Emily Smith would be Page Emily. If in doubt, you are never wrong to call any member of the Order as "Brother" or "Sister". It is expected that National Leadership is addressed by their proper title, but otherwise it is usually considered safe. Sergeant at Arms are referred to as Sergeant (Name). Knights are Sir (Name).

You should be aware of the nature of your circumstances. Are you "off duty" or "on duty?" That will help you know how to act.

ON–DUTY – Investiture Ceremonies, Conclaves, formal banquets, service projects, recruiting activities, fundraisers and other activities as designated by leadership. Be formal. Everything is by rank and title.

OFF–DUTY – Times of fellowship, prayer, priory meetings, social events and troop meetings. Be casual. Leadership is addressed by rank and everyone else can be brother/sister.

AT–EASE – There are moments when a leader can change the normal decorum and put you or everyone "at ease." When this happens, the formal etiquette is set aside and the parties can proceed on a personal and casual level.

Protocol and Chain of Command

Proper Chain of Command – As in the military, all members must strictly adhere to a Chain–of–Command discipline. If you have any issue within your Priory or Commandery, you should contact your Priory or Commandery Chaplain. He or she is there to ensure that everyone has an avenue to voice concerns and to provide guidance as appropriate.

Personal Friendship vs. Professional Brotherhood

Our Order places a large expectation upon its members to be true brothers/sisters to and for each other. It is strongly encouraged to establish personal friendships with other members.

You can be a personal friend of a member who outranks you. You will, however, need to keep in mind every moment whether you are On Duty or Off Duty. When you are "on duty", you must let your personal relationship take a back seat to the role your rank plays in the flow of duty. You should not expect special favors from having a friend of a higher rank. When "off duty", you can just be "brothers/sisters" and be at ease.

What if you do not like a fellow member? This happens. As much as we urge and promote unity and brotherhood, some people just may not like each other. You are not required to have all your fellow members on your friends list on Facebook and similarly, you do not need to socialize with them when off duty or during social events.

You ARE expected to maintain professional behavior at all times.

There is no excuse for rude or inappropriate demeanor. You must find a way to still work and serve with this person and not allow it to interfere with Priory affairs. You can always consult your Prior or the Chaplain for help in this.

We want you to make us a part of your life, but one in which it is in balance with all the other parts of your life. We want you to be an excellent parent/spouse/employee/church member. We do not want you to take anything away from those areas of your life. The expectations we place upon you can be easily done with only a minimal sacrifice of time. Yes, it will still be a sacrifice. We never have the time for new things. We must make time for the Order. The reward will be worth it!

We know you already lead a busy life. We do too! There are times when you will wonder how you can fit the Order in. We have all been there! However, it can be done! There is great reward to all the things we do as Templars. Whether it is something that benefits us directly or whether it is the opportunity to be there for someone when they really need you or touching the lives of those less fortunate than ourselves, there is a wonderful feeling that goes along with geting involved. These will not be wasted moments! They are moments you invest into a great return!

Here are some of the opportunities for participation in our Priory:

• Priory Meetings – Check with your priory for its schedule. Meetings are usually held once a month on a Saturday. They normally last 60–90 minutes and are conducted via video conferencing on Facebook. You can attend via PC, tablet, laptop, smartphone or any media allowing access to the internet. If you are present, it counts! If you are not present, the minutes are posted on the Priory page on Facebook within a day or two. If you read the minutes and then sign off in the comments "read and understood", that counts the same as if you attended the meeting itself!

• Troop Meetings – Not all priories have troops. Those that do hold meetings at a location that is normally within easy driving distance of where you live. It is expected that you will attend unless a valid reason prevents you. If something does happen where you cannot attend, you should contact your Troop Leader and be excused. The typical Troop meeting runs about 2 hours.

• Buddy Check – Those who choose to sign up for this are assigned to another member to be their "buddy". On the 13th of each month you contact each other to make certain that all is well. You are just there for each other to help lend a shoulder to lean on. Those who participate in this report that it makes a difference knowing that at least one person out there really knows you and is there for you when needed. Usually, this is only a one hour call per month.

• Service Work – Service work is scheduled well ahead of time and will occur at a particular location that will be announced well in advance. Service work is an important aspect of Templar life, so it is important that you make every effort to be involved in at least one project per year. Failure to participate in at least one event per year is a cause for serious concern.

Templar Academy of America

Through the Templar Academy of America, we have custom tailored courses for Templars of all ranks. These online courses are self–paced meaning there is no time requirement for completion. We do, however, recommend you give the training a high priority as you journey to Knighthood.

There are two places where training is very important: The Companion–at–Arms Corps and the Sergeant–at–Arms Corps.

The Companion–at–Arms Corps is where the new members begin their trip to Knighthood. Sharing the experience with Sister and Brother Templars side by side forges bonds that can last forever. In the Templar Academy of America courses for the Companion at Arms, the CAA will learn Templar history, the history unique to the OSMTJ–USA, what it means to be a Templar in all parts of life, and what the verbiage of the OSMTJ–USA is.

In the Templar Academy of America courses for the Sergeant–at–arms, the SAA will learn about the Virtues one must value, have, and live, to become a Knight. They will learn how to be a Leader, Sister, Brother and Templar.

Templar Academy of America Mission Statement:

To educate, train, and inspire each Templar to embrace and exercise their own God–given gifts and leadership style, so that each graduate is recognized as a person of integrity and character, committed to their Christian faith as lived through the Knightly Virtues, and prepared for excellence in dedication and service to their family, community, nation, priory, and the OSMTJ–USA.

As a part of your progression through the ranks and your initial training, all new members are required to complete an online course that will help you attain a better grasp for our values, and yours as well.

As part of your acceptance on the Templar path, you will be enrolled as a Templar Student in the Templar Academy at www.ktoa.org.

Completion of your studies is a requirement for advancement in each rank. Additionally, there is a six month probationary period on advancement for each rank, so it that students take their time in their studies rather than rush through for a desire for promotion.

Templar Round Table Discussion

Each week, a Templar Round Table Discussion is held on line using a preferred conferencing application. Please check the main channel to see the current application in use and connection instructions. We encourage all Brothers and Sisters to attend if at all possible.

OSMTJ KNIGHTS TEMPLAR OF AMERICA

These typically occur Thursdays at 11:00 AM PST / 2:00 PM EST.

Each week we have a new guest speaker who will share experiences of their walk with our Lord, discuss scripture and other topics of great interest. It's an excellent opportunity to "plug in" and take advantage of the life experiences and wisdom of others who love our Lord.

Each Round Table is approximately one hour in duration. The guest speaker shares his or her story for approximately 20 minutes and the balance of the hour consists of an open session with Q&A. It's an excellent way to experience fellowship with your Brothers & Sisters and add value to the lives of everyone.

The discussions are recorded and archived within the OSMTJ Facebook page for download should you want to miss it and want to listen.

Thank you for joining our most Holy Order. You are about to embark upon a wonderful journey that will surely make a difference in your life and the lives of those whom you touch. We look forward to you continued participation.

Of Symbols, Mottos, and Their Meanings

In the long history of our Order many symbols have become associated with it, some of which are approved and others which are not. To further confuse matters, the name Knights Templar has been co–opted by various other groups, such as Freemasons and Gnostics. The OSMTJ Knights Templar seeks at all costs to stay true to the spirit of the original knights, and will not allow the mingling of other beliefs.

Here we have listed several symbols and their meanings to serve as a guide to proper usage within the Order.

Approved Symbols:

Two Riders Seal: The Traditional Seal of the Knights Templar is an approved symbol. Depicting the spirit of the poor knights of Christ, two brothers share a horse. Legends say that Hugues de Payens and Godrey are the riders. The reverse side bearing the Temple Mount is also approved.

The Knights Templar.org

OSMTJ America Seal: This is the Seal of the modern Knights Templar of America. It bears the black and white battle standard of the Templars. The griffins represent strength and courage while the swords and shield represent

84

our spiritual battle and our very near divine protection. Above all is the crown of Divine Sovereignty.

Cross pattée: Frequently, but not exclusively, tied with the Templars, this cross is often represented on our mantles. Some have associated the splayed legs with a chalice or a candelabrum, representing the Grail or Light, respectively. This symbol became popular in heraldry and is often used atop the crowns of monarchs.

Chi Rho: This symbol traces its origin to the earliest chapters of Christianity, and is therefore not exclusively Templar in its usage, although they historically utilized it. It is a monogram of the two greek letters Chi (X) and Rho (P), which make up the first two letters of Christ in Greek (Khristos).

Jerusalem Cross: Also known as the Crusader's Cross, it is not Templar in origin, but rather was heraldry from the Kingdom of Jerusalem after its capture in the First Crusade. The Templars were created shortly after and there the association is often made. It is said to represent the five wounds of Christ or Christ and the four gospels or the four evangelists.

Templar Battle Flag: This is the banner the Templars carried into battle. The black represents the wicked world we have left behind while the white symbolizes our purity in Christ. The red cross stands for the sacrifice and martyrdom we may give for our God.

Disapproved Symbols:

Cross and Crown: The cross and crown is often associated with the Templars, but wrongly. It is only a symbol of the Templars within the ranks of Freemasonry. Additionally, it was used by the Bible Student Movement, which gave birth to the Jehovah's Witnesses, who deny the divinity of Christ.

Baphomet: Some of the heretical claims against the historical Templars included the worship of Baphomet. Early sources show this was a corruption of the name "Muhamet," the founder of Islam. It was then adapted by occultists and Satanists into their own mythos. This image was created by occultist Eliphas Levi.

Abraxas: Some inventive scholars have suggested that some Templars had connections to historical gnostic heresies, which may have included god/demon named Abraxas. Although some Abraxas seals have been found in association with the Templars, it seems it was used a symbol in heraldry, and was not an object of worship. No confessions or accusations of gnosticim ever arose from the tortures during  their inquisition. If there were any chance this accusation would stick, it surely would have been used.

Approved Mottos:

Non nobis, Domine, non nobis, sed Nomini tuo da gloriam: English: Not unto us, O Lord, not unto us, but unto thy Name give glory. This is a quotation from Psalm 115 that gives the proper humility and orientation for the aims of our Order.

Sigillvm Militvm Xpisti: English: Seal of the Army of Christ. This typically surrounds the historical seal of the Templars.

Pauperes Commilitones Christi Templique Salomonici: English: Poor Fellow Soldiers of Christ and the Temple of Solomon. This is a Latinized version of the full historical name for the Order.

Deus Vult: English: God Wills It. This motto is not distinctly Templar but finds its roots in the First Crusade to recapture Jerusalem. It is the Jerusalem connection that makes people associate it with the Templars. It may be used, but know that others use it for their own purposes and agendas.

Testis Sum Agni: English: I am Witness to the Lamb. This appeared on the seal of English Templars.

Neutral Stance Mottos:

In Hoc Signo Vinces: English: In This Sign Conquer. This motto is frequently used by Masonic Templars. Historically, it is a phrase that far predates the Templar era, as it was the words that Emperor Constantine I of Rome saw in his vision that converted him to Christianity. The Templar connection comes from the Templar Kingdom of Portugal. One of the most famous Templar Kings, King Alfonso Henriques, was praying the night before he would lead the Knights Templar on an attack on a Moorish stronghold in Portugal. As he was praying, This Templar King saw a sign from God blazed across the sky as clear as day: "IN HOC SIGNO VINCES." Full of confidence in Christ's sign, the Templar King won a major victory the next day at the Battle of Ourique (July 25th, 1139, the forces of Portuguese Afonso Henriques defeated the Almoravid Moors led by Ali ibn Yusuf).

This motto, therefore, has historical roots in the Templars, but since it has been co–opted by the Freemasons, it ought to be used with the aim of reclaiming it for our right and proper use.

A Rule of Thumb

One should recognize that the Templars are an Order of orthodox Christian beliefs. We believe in the divinity of Christ, the bodily resurrection of Christ, and the ultimate authority of the Scriptures. Should you find a symbol or motto not described here then do your research. One should not bear a symbol or motto that is infused with contrary beliefs or that might lead others to think improperly about what we represent. If still you are in doubt, feel free to ask someone in leadership for guidance.

Conclusion

Having laid a solid foundation within the Order through the study of this Introductory Manual, we charge you, poor fellow–soldier of Christ, to do your diligence to advance in your studies, to advance your brethren, and to advance the church of Christ for the glory of God. We are honored and pleased to receive of your participation in our most holy Order.

May God bless your endeavors as we work together for the Kingdom of Heaven. May you pursue this path with excellence and fervor so that none may have cause to gainsay this solemn way of life. May you use your talents and ambition not for merely your own good, but also for the good of the Order.

As you stand with us, we stand with you.

Non nobis, Domine, non nobis, sed Nomini tuo da gloriam.

Appendix
Priories of the Grand Priory of America

AL	St. Bernard	MI	St. Louis
AK	St. James	MN	St. Louis
AZ	St. Benedict	MS	St. Bernard
AR	St. Benedict	MO	His Coming Glory
CA	St. James	MT	St. Benedict
CO	St. Benedict	NE	St. Benedict
CT East	St. Michael	NV	St. James
CT West	St. Louis	NH	St. Michael
DE	Holy Cross	NJ	St. Louis
DC	St. Bartholomew	NM	Open
FL	St. Mark	NY	St. Louis
GA	St. Bernard	NC	St. Philip
HI	St. James	ND	St. Benedict
ID	St. Benedict	OH	St. Louis
IL	His Coming Glory	OK	St. Bernard
IN	His Coming Glory	OR	St. James
IA	St. Benedict	PA	Anne Askew
KS	His Coming Glory	PR	St. Mark
LA	St. Bernard	RI	St. Michael
ME	St. Michael	SC	St. Bernard
MD	Holy Cross	SD	St. Benedict
MA	St. Michael	TN	St. Bernard

TX		St. Gabriel
UT		His Coming Glory
VT		St. Michael
VA		St. Bartholomew
WA		St. James
WV		Holy Cross
WI		St. Louis
WY		St. Benedict

Commanderies

CT	West	Prince of Peace
FL	Miami	Santa Barbara
FL	Orlando	St. Ignatius
FL	Tampa	St. Lazarus
IL		St. Thomas
IN		St. Thomas
MI		The Apostles
NJ		St. Paul
OH		St. Polycarp
PA	East	The Trinity
PA	West	Lady Jane Grey
TN		St. Francis
WI		St. John

* This list is subject to change as new Priories and Commanderies are formed. This list is accurate as of the date of publication.

codex
spiritualis
press

Made in the USA
Monee, IL
31 March 2021